TALES FROM MANUS ISLAND

PAPUA NEW GUINEA

Geneva Ensign, *Editor*

TALES FROM MANUS ISLAND

ISBN #978-0-9953437-4-0

Copyright (c) 2021 Geneva Ensign

Printed in Canada by:
UBR Services Printing & Copies
9618-B Bottom Lake Road
Lake Country, British Columbia V4V 1S7
www.ubrservices.ca
2021

CONTENTS

Dedicated

to the long-ago

storytellers of Manus Island

and

to my children,

Greg

Geri

Grant,

who participated in this

adventure of a lifetime

with

enthusiasm.

Acknowledgements

IT IS NOT OFTEN that acknowledgements for assistance in publishing a book would span a fifty-year time frame, but the Manus Islanders, children and adults, who shared their legends and drawings did so long ago, in 1971!

A big debt of gratitude goes to many people. If my former husband, a sociology professor, had not been due a research sabbatical from the University of Alberta, I would never have attempted conducting my own Community Development research so far from home. I thank him for providing a unique opportunity and an adventure of a lifetime. Many of the photos were taken by him as well.

Our children, now grandparents themselves, Greg and Grant Kupfer and Geraldine Kupfer-Jennings, were enthusiastic participants in our adventure. Because talking with children is not as intimidating as talking with adults, our children often opened the door to many story-telling sessions with Islanders, young and old. Teenagers liked to give three-year old Grant a ride on their shoulders so they could practice their English with him. He heard many tales of masalai and monsters. Later, back at home in Canada, he wasn't always so sure that these same monsters were not hiding in his closet or under his bed.

I also wish to thank Rev. and Mrs. Norman Dietsch, Field Directors, Manus Evangelical Mission Station, for their generous hospitality. They, as well as their teachers and staff, enabled us in so many ways to conduct our research and to collect these tales.

I am especially indebted to the late Matthew Bill, the Mission's grade six Indigenous teacher, who trusted his classroom and his students with me. He not only facilitated the telling of the Manus tales so that I could record them, but he illustrated many of them with ink sketches. His art work is also on the cover of this book. I regret that he will not be able to read a book that he helped to create so long ago.

Many people have contributed to the compiling of these tales into book form. The members of the Westbank Writers' Group enthusiastically responded to a few of the legends that I read to them, encouraging me to publish. Two members of the Writers' Group were especially helpful. Joanne Lereaux graciously transposed the children's handwritten stories into a first draft, and Donna Bird, a co-facilitator of the Writers' Group, provided her excellent proofreading skills while making welcome editorial suggestions. Ursula Rymarchuk, of UBR in Winfield, British Columbia, did the final layout for the book and incorporated Matthew Bill's painting of a Manus canoe on the front cover.

One story, "Biboingangdri, A Bad Mama," had not been translated from Pidgin-English. The Rev. Norman Dietsch, now retired, translated it for the book. Pidgin-English terms were often used in the stories. When in doubt about the meaning, I used the website "Tok Pisin English Dictionary." Similarly, the names of villages are often spelled several different ways. I have referred to Google Maps usage.

Unfortunately, the children's illustrations had been drawn on gray construction paper. Mina Aiur and Heather Marnier, Technical Assistants, Westside Learning Lab, Okanagan

Regional Library, were able to lift the gray color so that the drawings could emerge more clearly. Crystal Williams did a final photo shopping and touch-up. Sadly, a few drawings remained a bit faded, but it was impossible not to include them. Through the eyes of Manus children, we get a glimpse of what it was like to be living on that tropical island fifty years ago.

Thank you all!

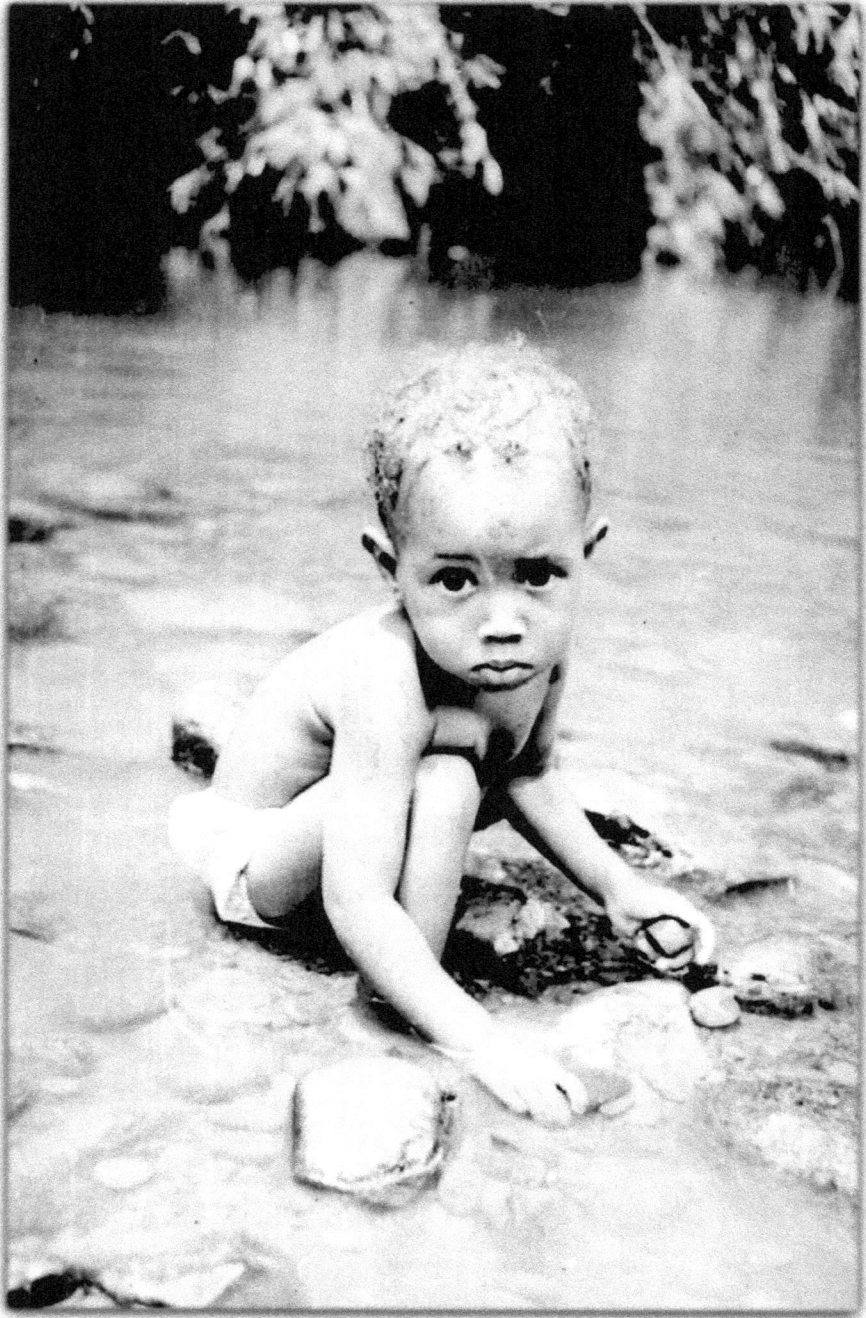

Introduction

THE YEAR WAS 1971.

Our plane slowly circled over the tiny airport. We saw from the window a ribbon of blindingly white coral, the road below snaking through unbelievably lush green coconut palms. Excited, we peered intently for our first glimpse of Manus, an island off the coast of Papua New Guinea. Then the airplane circled out over the bluest blue-green water, white coral reefs pushing up here and there. It is trite to say that the view was "too good to be true," nevertheless it was truer than true. I had wondered before our arrival here that perhaps we had painted our dreams of Manus Island much too vividly.

While studying the educational system in Papua New Guinea, a third world country on the verge of nationhood, my former husband and I, with our three little children aged six, five and three, would be living on a mission station belonging to the Lutheran Evangelical Church. Its field director, Rev. Norman Dietsch, had told us that Manus Island was the closest that a person could get to paradise while yet on this earth. No poisonous snakes, no mosquitoes, a mild climate, nearly always stable, and, when the rains did come, they were refreshing; the downpours washing everything clean. And downpours didn't last for long. Still, we had believed his view of his island paradise to be a bit biased.

As we carefully stepped down from the airplane on rickety make-shift stairs, a wave of humid, fragrant warm air immediately washed over us. Crushed coral led us along a winding path to and through the white wooden "in-gate." Neat and small, the airport. A white building was located to the side of white runways; everything was lined with coral gravel from the sea. Blinding whiteness in the intense sun.

After being officially recorded as visitors, our passports examined and stamped, we and our baggage were sorted, and we were on our way to discover for ourselves the island of Manus. The coral-graveled road wound past the edge of the blue-green sea, huge waves rolling again and again to the shore. The snow-white sandy beaches were even more beautiful than the Hawaiian ones we had recently enjoyed. Yet these beaches were empty; no one was surfing or sunbathing. There were no tourist facilities; in fact, tourism in the year of 1971 had not yet to come to the island. Tall coconut palm trees leaned gracefully over the road, providing welcome shade on this scorching hot ride to our temporary cinder block home.

My husband was on sabbatical from the Sociology Department at the University of Alberta, and I was conducting research on the role of Indigenous school teachers in preparing islanders for the upcoming Independence of Papua New Guinea from its Australian Protectorship. My research was to be focused on the conflicts arising when western-style education is used as a tool for development in an emerging nation.

Manus Island lies in the southwestern part of the Pacific Ocean. It origins are ancient; molten lava broke through the ocean's surface perhaps as many as eight to ten million years ago, leaving a series of scattered islands of which Manus is the largest. It is believed that human habitation dates back over fifty thousand years.

Many of the beliefs and customs of the people hark back thousands of years and are still practiced, even though they have had a series of colonizers, missionaries, teachers and government people trying to educate them in Western beliefs and practices. Manus Island was invaded by the Japanese during World War II and became the centre of fierce fighting before being liberated by American Forces.

While conducting my research on Manus Island, I also had the opportunity to informally learn about the customs and the culture, the Manus way of doing and seeing things. Many stories were told over tea and what they call biscuits in the little cinder block house that our family rented from the mission compound. As well, our research travels often took us by foot or by boat to remote village schools.

Whenever someone would tell me a story, usually in Pidgin-English, I would write it down and translate it with the assistance of Bilomon Bosiih, my friend and helper. It was fascinating to see traces of European contact incorporated into their legends, like a pussy cat going to visit the king or a government man trying to buy property from the villagers, or children running past the Momote airport while escaping from a masalai.

While there, I also taught classes in the local elementary school. One of the assignments for the sixth graders was to write and illustrate a Manus legend. When we returned to

Canada, I brought all the stories and pictures that I had collected, thinking to publish a book of legends which I could send back to the children in the Mission school.

Late in the year of 1972, I sat at my desk back in Edmonton, Alberta. I was writing my thesis on education and development in Papua New Guinea-- or trying to...

Instead, memories flooded. I saw Andrew, from Manus Island, walking toward me from the sea carefully carrying in his cupped hands a huge cowrie shell, a gift for me. I heard an old widow's voice quavering from behind her hut's wall, reciting for me an old legend, but not wanting me to see her. Images, one after another, paraded through my mind.

My thesis refused to become a scientific document. No matter how hard I tried to be academic, specific, terse, organized, professional, it revolted. The people of Manus Island came marching in—emotions on display, happy, laughing people, sad people, angry people...Boksep from Tingau, Nawes from Laues, Hikapet from Loniu, Bilamon from Lundret ...

I wanted to forget the thesis and, instead, write a treatise to life—to the whole person—to those Islanders who had not yet built their walls of sophistication around them, they who had not yet denied their innermost selves—their anger, their love, their spontaneity. They were not yet domesticated, made pliant, made lifeless.

Instead they had learned silence; had learned to wait and listen, to respond to the cues from the white man while in his presence. They withdrew or blossomed, depending how they were treated, being great readers of subtle cues, and sometimes not so subtle.

But duty called; my scientific thesis awaited, stripped as academically required of the colourful flavour of the Manus Island personalities. I tucked away the memories and the legends and got on with the business at hand—earning my Master's Degree in Community Development from the University of Alberta and to my subsequent career in Indigenous communities.

So now in 2021, exactly fifty years later, I am finally returning to Manus Island, not in person, but to my memories of long ago. On this tropical isle, palm trees beckon with outstretched arms; gentle breezes skip over the water. The rhythmic wash of the ocean on the sandy beach emphasizes a slow, unhurried pace of life.

Come, sit with me and listen to the voices of Manus Islanders sharing with us stories told and retold over the centuries. These age-old legends are filled with the stuff of life – death and birth, joy and fear, love and hate, monsters and masalai, as are their lives.

Let's listen.

PART I

Tales Told By Manus Island Adults And Teens

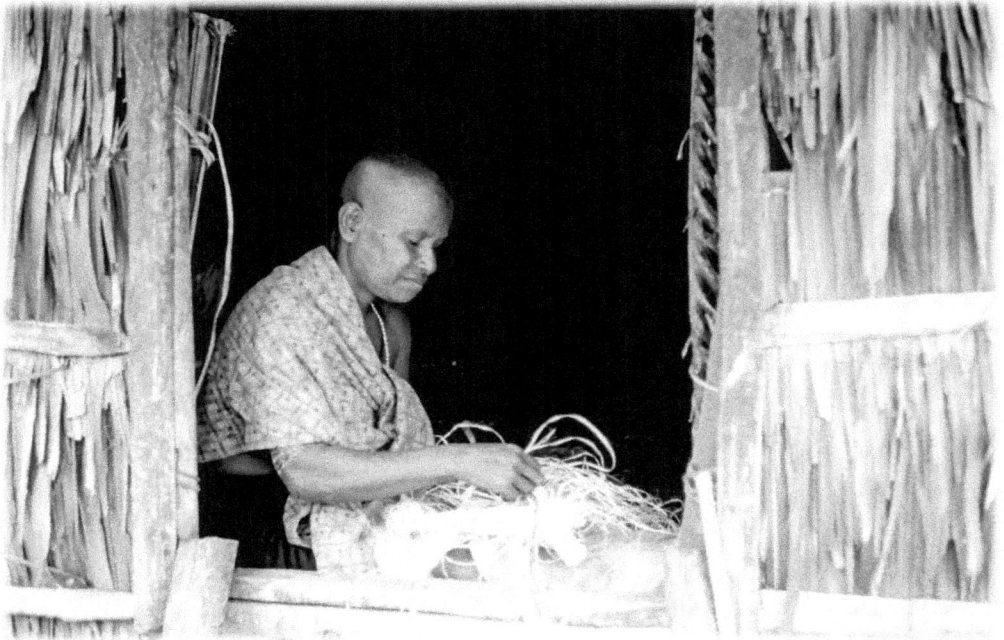

A Foolish Old Woman
And Her Old Husband

A long time before, there lived on the island of Manus an old, old woman, Bibondu, and her old, old husband, Bondromi. The two of them lived peacefully—or fairly so—in a small house not far from the beach and not far from the bush.

One day old Bondromi said to his old wife, "Meri bilong me, I am hungry for some meat to go with our sak sak. You and I will go to the bush this morning to find a cus cus."

Bibondu was cross. She was very cross indeed as she scolded, "Oh husband of mine, I am very old. You do not have eyes to see me anymore. You do not look at me. Can you not see that my legs are not strong? They pain. My arms are not strong. They pain. I am not able to walk about to find cus cus!"As she wailed her complaints, she waved her arms which were wrapped around in ragged and dingy pieces of lap lap, as were her legs.

But Bibondu was deceiving her husband. As soon as her weary man, Bondromi, had slowly hobbled down the path and into the bush without her, Bibondu unwrapped the pieces of lap lap and scurried around the tiny room. Arm bands, carefully woven from bush materials, were placed around her arms; a new grass skirt was fastened around her waist. From the blackened clay oil pot hanging from the rafters above the open fire, she poured oil over her wrinkled breasts, arms and face. Her dogtooth necklace she tied carefully around her neck and completed her preparations by brushing red paint into her hair. Magically enough, Bibondu looked young again.

Pleased with herself, she walked quickly to the beach where a young man, Kabul, was standing waist deep in the blue green waters of the lagoon; his spear was poised to throw. Bibondu sang out to him, "Kabul, Kabul. Bring one fish to me."

Now when Kabul heard Bibondu call, he was pleased. He selected the nicest fish from the group that he had tied together in the salt water and tossed it onto the white sand. Wading to Bibondu over the coral, Kabul cut a tiny hole in the belly of the fish expertly, and with agility, extracted the intestines. Rinsing the fish in the salt water, he gave it to Bibondu.

Bibondu took the fish and carried it carefully, slowly returning up the winding path to the tiny house. Satisfied that Bondrami was still in the bush looking for cus cus, she quickly removed her arm bands, the dogtooth necklace, the new grass skirt and hid them high in the cross bars of the rafters. She washed the red paint from her hair and rubbed her skin until the oil vanished and the familiar wrinkles reappeared. Around her arms and legs she again wound the dirty, frayed pieces of lap lap.

Lapun once more, she cooked the fish with taro. Bibondu ate her meal with great satisfaction, putting aside a tiny, tiny piece of the tail of the fish and a tiny, tiny piece of taro in the black wooden food dish, the lus. When Bondrami arrived home, tired from his unsuccessful day of hunting, he said, "Meri, bilong me. I am very hungry. What can I eat?"

Bibondu slowly reached for her walking stick. Hoisting herself up from the mat, she hobbled to the fire where Bondrami's food waited. With a great show of effort, she handed him the tiny bits of fish and taro which were almost lost in the big wooden lus. But Bondrami did not complain. When he finished, he said quietly, "I liked the fish, Bibondu. Who gave it to you?"

And again, Bibondu lied, "The children, that's who. They gave me the fish." The old couple slept. The next morning Bondrami tried again, "Bibondu, you and I must go to the bush. Today we will find a cus cus to eat. We have not had meat for a long time."

And again, Bibondu raged at her old husband, "I am old—finished. My legs are not strong. They pain. My arms are not strong. They pain. I am not able to walk about looking for food. You do not have eyes. You do not look at me." Her bandaged arms waved in the air as she complained loudly.

So again Bondrami went alone to the bush in search of meat for the two of them. Watching him disappear down the path, the old woman schemed to go again to the beach in search of Kabul. Bibondu carefully decorated herself with all the bilas she had hidden the day before. From the oil pot came the coconut oil to smooth out the wrinkles, and, as if by magic, her skin looked young once more.

Returning to the beach, she found her fisherman in the same spot as the day before. She sang out to him in her most alluring voice, "Kabul, Kabul. Get one fish and come to me." Kabul selected another fine fish and brought it to her.

Meanwhile, Bondrami had come back to their house to find his old wife. Bondrami searched everywhere for her. She was not in the house. She was not in the garden. Along the winding path he came, searching for her—until he came to the beach. There Bondrami saw his wife, Bibondu, and Kabul talking together as Kabul cut and cleaned the fish.

Bondromi looked at Bibondu. He looked. He saw the ragged pieces of lap lap were gone from her arms and from her legs. He looked. He saw the arm bands, the red paint, the new grass skirt, the necklace of dog teeth. He looked. He saw her shining skin, rubbed with coconut oil and gleaming in the bright sun light. Rage flooded him as he looked and saw this wife of his, too old to hunt for food, now standing with a young man on the beach.

Bondromi shouted at her, "Before, I asked you to go with me to the bush to find meat and you—you said you were too old! Your legs were not strong. They pained. Your arms were not strong. They pained. You were not able to walk about. When I wanted to come home to you, you were not in the house. You were not in the garden; you were not on the path. You have come to the beach. Look at you! You come to your yangpela man and now you are talking with him!"

In his blind jealousy and rage, Bondrami grabbed a piece of driftwood lying on the white sand and brought it down on the head of his woman, the old wife that belonged to him. Red paint and blood intermingled as she died there on the sand.

The man, Kabol, he ran away.

Storyteller: Bisindra from Tingau, a seventy years old woman. Told to her by her mother, and told to her mother by her mother's grandmother.

At first Bisindra was shy about telling the story, protesting, "Mi no inap long stori!" But after a time, she disappeared behind the verandah wall, and soon a quavering voice began to tell the story with relish. The tone of her voice revealed her enjoyment of the foolish secrets of another lapun meri of long ago. She used a sing song voice for the parts where Bibondu complains to her husband that he has no eyes to see her and changed to a soft musical tone where Bibondu sings out to her prospective lover, Kabol, to bring her a fish.

The Girl Who Left Her Mother

Long ago, there was a girl who lived with her mother. In the olden days, a girl who is fifteen or sixteen cannot work for three or four days every month. One day her mother went to the market to buy some taro. As she was alone at home and she was hungry, she took her mother's food and ate it. When her mother came home, she asked her daughter, "Who ate my food?"

So the girl said, "Oh Mother, I ate your food." Her mother was angry with the girl. The girl was sad; she took a bag and went away to find a new mother.

On her way, she came to a house near the river. She went to the house to ask for help. An old man came to the door. He asked her, "Where do you come from?"

She told the old man, "I was living with my mother, but I did something very bad so my mother is mad at me."

The man said, "Well, Girl, sit down and have some taro and fish." But it was not taro and fish; it was pig meat, which was only eaten at special times. For about four weeks, the girl stayed with the old man.

One day the girl told the old man that she must go and so he gave her some Manus baskets and she went away. She walked and walked until she came to a very big hill. It was very high up. There she stayed.

Now if you walk from Lugos to Buliso, you may see the mountains which are above the Tingau River. There are coconut trees and wild wood flowers which she planted there.

Storyteller: Sarah Pokio from Buliso.

Thirty Men Captured By A Masalai

Long ago there were thirty men. They lived in the village of Naues. One day, the thirty men from the village went to sea to catch some fish. They stayed there for several days, cooking and sleeping on the canoe.

There was a masalai in the area who turned himself into a huge fish. Flapping his tail around, he put out their fire on the canoe. The fire was made from the coconut palm leaves. Then the men were without fire and could not cook their food.

Later as they looked at the nearby beach, they saw a fire. The leader of the men selected one man. He said to him, "You must go ashore and light a torch from that fire and bring it to us so that we may have fire again."

The man swam to the shore. As he was lighting the torch, a masalai came out. He said, "You must stay here with me and warm yourself by my fire. It is cool." Then the man sat down and warmed himself.

The leader waited and waited for the first man to return. When he did not come back, he sent another man to bring back the fire. Again, the masalai said, "You must stay here with me awhile and warm yourself." The man sat down and warmed himself and did not return to the canoe.

One by one the thirty men were sent for fire only to remain with the masalai. When they were all there, including the leader, the masalai said, "Come, you must stay in my house.

I will go with some of my friends and we will beat sago for you to eat."

When the masalai returned in the afternoon, he told the men that he had no sago yet and then he went away again. The masalai was really telling lies to the men because he wanted to save the sago to eat when he made a feast of the thirty men.

The men, however, thought he was a good man and waited a long time for the sago he promised. After a very long time, the leader became impatient and turned himself into a little bird. He flew around until he saw the masalai beating sago. He flew near and began to cry. The masalai said, "Why are you crying? I am beating sago and am going to make a feast of the thirty men in my house. You should not cry."

The bird flew away and came back to his people as a man. He told the twenty-nine men what he had heard. He said that they must build a large canoe. They must put an outrigger on it and make a large paddle. They worked hard and the leader showed them how to make the paddle and fasten the outrigger onto the canoe. By early morning, they launched the canoe and began to paddle away quickly.

When they saw the sun rise, the masalai and his friends were ready to eat the thirty men. When they arrived at the house, thirty men had already gone. The masalai ran to the beach, only to see the thirty men on the ocean in their new canoe.

Seeing the masalai, the leader called, "Why don't you cut a long bamboo and put one end on the beach and the other end on our canoe?" In his anger, the masalai did what the leader suggested and when the masalai was walking on the bamboo, the men chopped the bamboo in two.

The masalai fell down into the ocean where the sharks and crocodiles ate his body.

Storyteller: Nahina Pokop from Laues. Told to her by her grandmother.

The Cat And The Mouse Go To Sea

One day the sea was very calm so the cat and the mouse wanted to go for a paddle in the sea. The cat sat at the back and the mouse sat in front.

While they were paddling, they saw two pretty girls walking along the beach. As they passed by, the cat told the mouse, "Hey, Dear Mouse, I want to marry the girl who is wearing the banana leaf!"

But the mouse said, "No, I want to marry her."

Both of them wanted to marry the same girl. They argued for a long time. The mouse got sick of so much talking so he gnawed a hole in the bottom of the canoe. Both of them sank into the sea. The mouse swam to the beach, but the cat could not swim and he drowned.

Storyteller: Sarah Pokio from Buliso.

How Chaplacki Saved Ten Women

One day in the village of Loniu, ten of the women decided to go to the garden. They went and pulled their canoe down to the sea and paddled off toward the Loniu Bridge. When they reached the bridge, they pulled up the canoe onto the beach. They walked over the worn path through the bush and started to make their new garden.

When it was getting late afternoon, they said to each other, "We will go home now." They packed their tools and walked back down the path to the bridge. When they came to the bridge, they saw Cheenin, a masalai, standing there. Cheenin was a huge masalai, an evil spirit, and they were very frightened.

Cheenin said to the women, "Come with me and we will go to my house."

The ten women said, "No, we want to go and see our families."

But Cheenin said, "I will take you to my house, and tomorrow I will take you back to the village." So they had to go with him. When they got to the house, they were horrified to see the bones of many people strewn around the house. They looked at each other and began to cry.

Early in the next morning, Cheenin woke up and went out, locking the door behind him. He found his masalai friend and told him, "I have ten women there in my house. I want you to go with me to beat the sago and we will have a feast." The two went to prepare the sago to go with their fine feast.

Now nearby the house of Cheenin, an old old woman named Chaplacki lived high up in a tree. When she heard the women crying in the house, she cried out in her magic words, "If this house is my house, the door will open." The door did open and Chaplacki hurried the ten women up the tree where she lived.

Soon Cheenin came back and, seeing the door open, called out, "Are you in the house?" Nobody answered him. Then he looked up into the tree and saw the ten women. He ran to his house to get his bush knife and axe to cut down the tree. But all of his bush knives and axes were broken.

Chaplacki let a vine down from the tree and called, "Cheenin, if you want the women, you can climb the vine and come up." As he climbed, Chaplacki hacked the vine with her knife and Cheenin fell down and died. Quickly they put the ladder to the ground and they carried him near to his house. They cut open his stomach and took out his heart. When they put it on the frying pan, it was no good, leva belong em I nogut.

The Chaplacki told the ten women, "I'll send you back home, but you must bring me two white pigs." Then she sent them home. They were happy to see their families again and later they brought one white pig and one black pig. Chaplacki was very angry. She said, "I don't want your black pig. Carry it home again!" And so Chaplacki lived in her house in the bush tree.

But when the women wanted to go to the bush to make a garden again, they remembered Cheenin, the masalai, and Chaplacki who was unhappy with them. So they stayed in their houses and did not go to the bush to make gardens anymore.

Storyteller: Hikabet from Loniu. Told to her by her aunt.

How The Betel Nut Came To Manus

Once upon a time there was a small boy who lived with his grandfather and grandmother. They did not look after him carefully. Then he went to a big tree beside the beach. He took one seed and talked to it with magic words. The seed opened. The boy went inside the seed. Then the seed fell down in the sea.

The seed drifted far away in the ocean. It went to an island where there were women on the beach finding shells. One woman was close to the seed and the boy cried out inside the seed. The woman heard him cry and looked over all the seeds. At last she found the seed with the boy inside. The woman picked up the seed and the boy came out of it.

He walked with the woman and they went to her house. The woman cooked some food and gave it to him. Then she took a betel nut and leaf and gave it to him and he chewed it. The boy said, "This betel nut is not good; it doesn't get red."

The boy took the knife and an axe. He went to the bush and climbed the betel nut and cut some leaves. He shared them with the men in the Loniu village on Manus. When they started to chew, the leaves became red. Then they made a big feast for the clever boy who had brought the betel nut to them from Rambutcho Island.

Storyteller: Nawes from Laues. Told to her by her grandmother from Rambutcho Island.

The Mango Tree

A long time ago a man lived in a village. He had nine children. There was very little food to eat, but near their house was a large mango tree. When the tree was full of fruit, the man took a basket and climbed up the tree. He picked all of the mangoes and climbed down again.

He got down, but one son had spotted another mango left in the very top of the tree. He told his father to climb back up again and get the mango. While he was climbing the tree, the mango fell down to the ground. His boys were searching for it and before they could find it, the mango turned into a boy. Everyone was surprised but accepted him and he became another son of the family.

Now this man had many children and they were always hungry; they used to eat a bag of sago every day. Their mother became angry because they ate so much food. So she told her husband to take them to the bush. The boys carried some baskets of sago and some knives and followed the father to the bush. The mango boy was coming last in line.

Their father told them to look for a tree to chop down for a canoe. They saw a nice tree and they started to chop it down. While they were chopping it down, the father said, "I will go and hunt birds for dinner." Then he went away, but he tricked them and went home.

When the mango boy climbed a tree, he saw the sun was going down. The children took sago from the basket and ate it. Then they walked home, following the mango boy. As they came near the village, they were singing and shouting. The mother heard all the noise and was angry with her husband.

The children came home, ate their dinner and went to sleep. Early in the morning, the woman cooked food for them again. The children and the father, they all went to the bush. Again, while they were walking to the bush, the mango boy was the last. They finished chopping the tree down and the father said he would hunt birds for dinner. Again, he tricked them and went home. While they were chopping more sago, the mango boy climbed up again and saw the sun go down. They ate the sago and went home.

When their mother heard their singing and shouting, they knew she was very angry, but she cooked them some food and they went to sleep. Next morning, again the mother cooked sago, put it in their baskets and they went to the bush. While they were chopping the canoe, the father said he would hunt birds for dinner. Again he tricked them and went home.

When the mango boy climbed up the tree, he noticed the sun was going down. When it was time to go home, they could not find the way. It became very dark and they were still in the bush. When they were wandering around, trying to find the way home, they saw a house. They saw a man who called to them, "Come."

They were tired from the long day and they went in the house. Now they did not realize that this was really the house of a masalai. Before they slept, he gave a red lap lap to all the boys and gave white lap laps to all his own sons. They lay down to sleep.

While they were sleeping, the mango boy stood up and told his brothers to run away. While they were running away, the masalai woke up, took his sword and chased the fleeing boys. When the masalai came close to them, they saw a stone near the road. The mango boy said the magic words, "If it is the masalai's stone, it will not open but if it is our stone, it will open." When he had said the magic words, the stone opened and the children went inside. The stone closed again.

The masalai came and started to dig a hole near the stone, but he could not and he finally gave up and went to sleep. When they saw he was asleep, they took his sword and ran away. While they ran, the masalai woke up, but the masalai had no strength to chase them so he went to his house. The boys went back to their mother and father's house and they were very happy.

One day they were in the village and they began to shoot each other with stones. They divided into two groups. The mango boy hit a small boy with a stone and he began to cry. The boy's mother was very angry with the mango boy. The mango boy was sad.

The mother cooked sago and most of them went for a walk, but the mango boy only sat under the house. He told his brothers that he was going to go back to the mango tree. So he climbed up to the very top and he is still there, a mango.

Storyteller: Maien from Loniu. Told to him by his father who was told by a relative from Rambutcho Island whose his father had told him.

How The Bipi People Left Loniu For Another Place

One time a long time before, all the people who now come from Bipi Island lived in the Loniu Village of Manus Island. The Loniu people did not have fire. Every time they needed fire, they would call for it from the Bipi people. One day when the Loniu people wanted to make a garden, they again called for fire from the people of Bipi.

The Bipi people were unhappy and said, "We are tired of you calling for our fire. We want to find a new place to live." The Loniu people did not want their source of fire to go away, so there was a big fight. The Loniu people won, but the Bipi people ran away anyway.

They went down to the north coast of Manus and stayed on what became known as Bipi Island. Still today, when they speak their language and we speak ours, it is the same language. Some of the Bipi people came from Loniu, Papitalai, Narrangel and Makarin.

Storyteller: Hikabet from Loniu. Told to her by her mother.

The Bamboo Flute

A long time ago a man lived in the middle between Narrangel and Loniu. The man planted a big garden and was very happy. One day he took his bamboo flute to the garden and played it for a time. Then he put it up in a tree and began to work his garden. Meanwhile, two sisters from Rambutcho Island were walking along the beach looking for clams. They heard his beautiful song from the flute. The oldest sister said, "Sister, listen. What is that?"

The youngest sister said, "I think it is a bamboo flute playing on the mountain."

The oldest sister said, "Come, let us go and search for it!" They listened and followed the sound of the flute up the mountain. The man had put down the flute and was working again. He did not see the two women take the flute from the tree. They ran back down the mountain and paddled away in their canoe towards Rambutcho Island.

The man had a strange feeling; he said, "Where is my flute now? Maybe it's gone!" When he looked for the flute, it was not there in the tree. He hurried to the beach; he saw the two women paddling their canoe quickly away. He thought that they must have his flute. He pulled his canoe into the water and paddled after them.

But the women had begun sooner and they paddled so hard that they were far ahead of him. They paddled to an island and hid in a nearby cave. When the man reached the beach, the two women called to him, "What are you coming here for?"

He answered, "I have come here to take my flute!" The women did not answer, but they ran away further.

He called, "If you are my mother, bring my flute back."

They said, "We are not your mother."

He called again, "If you are my sister, bring my flute back."

They answered, "We are not your sister."

Again, he called, "If you are my brother, bring my flute back."

He tried many kinds of relatives, but each time, they answered, "We are not."

Finally the sisters became angry and broke his flute into pieces and threw them back to him. He took all the pieces and went back to the canoe. On the way home, he came near an island. On the island he saw a big woman masalai and her child. She called to him. "Come and wash our child."

He said, "Our child! How did I come to you and give you that child?"

The masalai said, "Come," but he only came to the edge of the beach and left his canoe there. When he wanted to go home, the masalai chased him. He climbed a tree and the masalai followed. He jumped on another tree and another until his lap lap caught on the branch of a tree. The masalai caught him, poked his eyes out and threw him to the ground. Then she came down and took out his armpits.

She left him for dead and looked for her baby. The waves had washed coral over the baby and it was dead. She took it and went home. The waves washed over the man lying on the beach and the birds made excreta on top of him. He was left there alone.

The two women who stole his flute were paddling by and saw him lying there. They put his body inside a karoke, a rain mat made from pandanas leaves, and held it up with a stick.

The older sister said to the younger one, "You stay and look after the man." The older sister left.

After a while, the man threw his arms in the air and the stick fell down. In a little while, he moved his leg and the other stick fell down. Slowly he woke up and he was afraid. He started to run away.

"Come back," said the younger sister. "Why do you want to run away?"

"No, I can't come back, "said the man, "I am afraid of the masalai." But he did come back and told her the whole story.

The younger sister called to her big sister. When she came to the shore, she heard the story too. They both said, "Come, let us go to our home and we will take care of you."

But the man said, "No, we will go to my home." When the man was strong again, they went to his home. The three of them were married and lived happily in Puwas, in the middle between Narrangel and Loniu.

Storyteller: Dora Hiyoweh from Loniu. Told to her by her grandfather.

How The Sailfish Came
To Manus Island

One day near Los Negros Island, there lived an old woman by herself in a village. One day she wanted to make a basket. She went to the bush to get the bark of the tree from which to weave the basket. While she was getting it, she cut herself with a seashell. She caught the blood in a coconut shell and hung it on the roof of her house.

Every day she watched it. One day in her coconut basket she discovered a big round egg and another that was long and small. She watched the two eggs closely every day. One day, the eggs finally cracked and out of the big round egg came an eagle and from the long, small one came a snake.

The old woman was delighted. Now she had someone to live with her, two people that she could care for. She became their grandmother and they grew up.

When they were big, the grandmother was old now and every day the snake and the eagle went to the bush to find food for themselves and for the old woman too. Every day the eagle brought back food to share, but the snake would eat all of what he found.

The eagle and the grandmother became unhappy with the snake. So every day when the eagle flew to the bush to find food, he would look for a good tree for them to live in, somewhere away from the snake. He flew a long way over the water and one day he found a good tree. He killed a pig and brought it to the grandmother. Because the snake was so greedy, they left without telling him. The old lady sat inside her house and the eagle took hold of the house and flew high in the air, putting the house down in a tree far away. But their food was getting scarce and it was difficult to find.

Meanwhile, when the snake had come home from the bush, he was surprised to find the house was gone. He looked all around, but he could not see the house or the old woman or the eagle. He tried to make magic to find where they were. He smelled the wind in all directions—south, north, east, west. When he said the magic words, chewed the beetle nut, spit and said more magic words, he saw that the grandmother and the eagle were in the east toward Rambutcho.

Then he started to swim to them. When the eagle saw him, he told the old woman and she sharpened her knife. When the snake climbed up the tree, the grandmother took the knife and cut its head off. The snake died. The grandmother told the wind and the rain to fall down and wash the snake into the open sea.

Every day the eagle searched for food for them. One day the eagle found a place—Tubat on the north coast—where many people from the village were beating sago. When they had gone, he flew down and took some. He did this several times. The people noticed that their supply of sago was decreasing. One day they hid themselves around the sago and watched. While they were there, the giant eagle came down; he pushed over the cover of sago leaves from the bags of sago and took four bags in one claw and four in the other.

The people were furious, and as he flew away, the people threw sticks and stones at him. One old crooked man with a twisted leg threw up his stick and broke the bones of one of the eagle's wings.

The eagle flew on. The one wing hung limp and useless; the other wing was flapping furiously to try to stay aloft. People on a small island about the size of Lugos were busy building houses of sago. They saw the huge eagle overhead and the flapping of his wing created a great wind which blew the sago leaves high into the air. As they watched in amazement, they saw the eagle fall to the shores of a nearby island. Hurriedly they dragged their canoes into the sea and paddled toward the island where the eagle had fallen.

They put him into their canoe and paddled back to their own village. They were surprised when the eagle spoke to them. "Do not kill me. I can help you. If your enemy wants to come and fight you, you must put me in a little house. When I die, you keep my bones there. When you fight you must carry pieces of my bones in your pocket and when you fight, you will always win. But you must bury the rest of me."

One day the eagle died. The people of the village all mourned the death of their friend. Later the place called Tubat, where the eagle had stolen the sago, sent out the men to fight the village people. They all ran to the little house and took pieces of bones and began to fight their enemy. At the end of the battle, the Tubat people had been defeated.

The Tubat people were puzzled. They could not figure out why the village people had been so strong. One old man said, "What have these people got—some special magic? Why can they kill our fighters and we cannot kill theirs?"

Another old man had a good idea. He said, "A woman from our village must go and marry a man from their village. She must find out what special magic they use and get some and send it to our village."

Just as they had planned, a woman was sent to marry a young man of the village. She discovered the secret of the eagle's bones and sent some back to her village. The people were happy, saying, "This time we shall win the war." They took their weapons and invaded the tiny village.

But, since both villages had the bones of the eagle, neither side could win. They all fought to the death, completely destroying all the inhabitants of both villages. When the rains came and washed the snake into the open sea, as the grandmother had asked, the snake changed into a long fish, which sometimes yet jumps out of the sea and skips along on his tail. That is how the first sailfish came to Manus Island.

Storyteller: Lihiu from Loniu. Told to him by his mother. Lihiu's friends, Sioni, Silan, Nosem, Pangai, Porek, Keheng, and Peter Lele, helped him tell the story, conferring together and adding their special interpretations from Pidgin English into English.

Two Brothers And How One Was Killed

It was a nice day and two brothers were having a walk on the beach. Their mother and father died soon after they were born. They were happy in their village; they had a good house and a good life, but the two of them had no wife to help them cook and do the washing.

One fine day, the oldest brother went to the beach to have his bath. While he was bathing, a stone hit the water beside him with a splash. He looked around quickly, but no one was there.

Then some stones fell into the water again, so again he looked around. He saw two girls standing on the beach. He called to them and they came to him. He took them both off to his house and the two brothers married them.

One day the younger brother went to the garden to get some kau kau. There the army man came and killed him and cut him in half. His food was ready and his wife was waiting for him to come back, but the sun was nearly down and everything was dark. At night the moonlight was so nice and the sky was clear. The oldest brother went out to look for him. He called and he called again and again, but he got no answer.

Soon he saw his brother. He was hanging up in a tree. He was so sad. He climbed up and got his brother down and carried him back to the village. He married his brother's wife. He had two wives from then on.

Storyteller: Sarah Pokio from Buliso.

The Pussy Cat Visits The King

Once upon a time, there was a pussy cat who made a garden. One night while he was sleeping, the village people came and stole his crops. He was very mad.

One day the King of England wrote a letter to all the villages. It said, "Nobody is allowed to steal—at night or in the daytime! If a person steals, he will be put in the calaboose." So the cat made another garden again. He planted watermelon in the garden. One day he decided to take one of his watermelons and give it to the King.

He carried the melon to the wharf at Lorengau and waited for a ship. One ship came in and he asked the captain, "Can I come in the ship and go with you to England?"

The captain said, "I have no space for you." Another ship came and still they did not let him on.

Finally the last ship came and again he asked the captain, "Can I come in the ship and go with you to England?"

The captain said, "Yes, there is room for you."

While he was on board, the captain said, "If you go to the King's palace, there are many soldiers there. Don't be afraid if they try to kill you." He arrived in England. When he was walking along the road to the King's palace, he saw his face in a mirror, a magic mirror.

When he knocked on the door of the palace, the King let him in and let him sit on a chair. The pussy cat said to the King,

"I am still here so you have to cut my watermelon and have a piece."

When the King cut the watermelon, money poured out all over the King's palace. When it filled all the inside of the palace, it poured outside. The King told his servants to collect all the money.

The King had two daughters. He asked the first born if she would like to marry the pussy cat. She said, "He is a cat; I won't marry him!"

Then the King asked the second daughter if she would like to marry the cat. The second daughter said, "If he is a cat or if he is a man, I will marry him." And so they were married.

One day the King made a big feast. He said, "Whatever man will win the race, he will marry my first born daughter." On the night of the games, the King's family went to watch. The cat told his wife to go with her parents to see the game.

When they were gone to sit on the chairs, the cat changed himself into a man. He cleaned his magic mirror with his lap lap and there he saw a horse. He jumped on the horse and rode to where the games were being held. His horse stood outside the brick wall. When they started to count all the horses for the race, his horse jumped over the wall and began to race with all the others. It ran fast and beat all the other horses. No one knew who the strange winner was. When the King's family came home, the pussy cat asked, "Who won the race?"

The King said, "One man won the race, but he disappeared from us." The King called another race, and again the strange man won the race. This time as he disappeared, the second daughter heard him laugh and she recognized the laugh! It was her husband. It was her secret. She told no one, but went quickly by herself to look for the cat skin before her husband could come home and change back into a cat again. She found the skin and burned it.

When she told the King that the winner was her cat husband who had changed into a man, her older sister heard it too. The first born daughter said to the King, "I want to marry this man as you promised."

The second daughter cried, "Oh no! At first our father, the King, asked you to marry the cat, but you refused. You said he was only a cat and you didn't want him. He is my husband now."

The King said to the man, "You will become King and my second daughter will become a queen. We, my queen and I, will be your servants."

Storyteller: Nahina Pokop from Laues.

The Huge Snake

One beautiful day a young girl was walking along the path to the garden. She was singing as she went. Far above in the top of a coconut tree, there was a bird's nest. She climbed that tree because she wanted to take the nest. As she was climbing up to the nest, she saw a gigantic snake. The snake had wanted the bird's nest, but now the snake was ready to jump on her.

She quickly climbed back down the tree and stood on the ground, looking at the snake carefully. When the snake started to come down the tree to kill her, she was very frightened and ran as fast as she could to her village. She ran to her house to tell her father about the snake. Then her father asked, "Where is the snake?"

"Over there on the main road," she answered. She went back with her father to kill the big snake.

When they got there, the girl showed the snake to the father. She said to her father, "Look! The snake is there, sitting on the branch of that tree."

Then her father said, "I saw it already." He climbed up the casuarina tree and fought with the snake for a long time. Finally, it fell down out of the casuarina tree and died.

They both went home. The girl was very happy. Her parents told her never ever to walk under that casuarina tree again!

Storyteller: Anna Bisau-u from Lihai.

The Old Grandmother

Once there was an old grandmother who had two grandchildren, a boy and a girl. They lived happily together in the village. One day the grandmother had to go away. She wanted to be sure her grandchildren would be good while she was away. So she told them to get the legs of a dead man and hang them from a beam in the ceiling of their house.

When the grandmother went away, the legs began to talk. They said, "If you two are not good, we will eat your food." The children were very frightened, but the boy ran to get his spear and, while the legs were still talking, he shot them with the spear.

When the grandmother came home, she was very angry. She told them to go to the bush and bring her some thorns from the thorn tree. They did. Then the grandmother pretended to look for lice in the children's hair, but she really rubbed their foreheads to make them sleep. They fell sound asleep and, while they were sleeping, she took the thorns and scratched big sores into their bodies. Then she carried the boy to the river and threw him in.

The boy swam to a large rock in the water and climbed up on it. When he stood up, he said, "Where is my sister?" Suddenly his sister appeared in front of him; he held onto her hair until he could see the rest of her.

They stayed on the rock, falling asleep. The girl dreamed of a banana. When she woke up, she told her brother her dream.

He said that he had seen a banana before she told him of her dream. He told her, "I saw a little banana over there before. Maybe it's ripe." The banana was ripe when they went to see; they cut it down with a stone and ate it.

Later the boy told his sister, "You stay here. I will go to the village and see if I can find some more fruit for us." The boy found a garden with many kinds of fruit. One time he brought bananas, another time pineapples, another time sap sap.

One time as he was taking a pineapple, a man grabbed him and said, "You are stealing my fruit!" He told the boy that he must stay with him. The boy did, but he didn't tell him about his sister.

The man was a good hunter. Sometimes he would bring a cus cus; sometimes a pig for the boy to cook. The boy would cook it and eat some of it. Then he would carefully wrap some parts with leaves and mix it with the rubbish. He carried the rubbish then to the bank of the river and threw it near the water. The girl would wait for this, get the meat when the brother left and eat it.

One day the man said to the boy, "I always kill big pigs and cus cus, but I never get much to eat. Where do you put all the meat? Do you eat it all or throw it away?"

Then the boy said, "I give it to my sister." Then the boy told the man all about his sister and the grandmother. The man was kind. He told the boy to go and get his sister. He went and brought her to the village. They stayed with the man and grew up to be big.

One day the man decided to give a big sing sing in their honour. The grandmother heard about it and came to the party. They boy and girl sent her away, saying, "You go away. You did not want us. We do not want you."

So she went away without eating any food or talking to them.

Storyteller: Nawes from Laues.

Kut, The Octopus, And The Children

A long time ago before the present time, there was an octopus that lived in the sea. Its house was a rock situated in the sea between Lusa and Lorengau near the mouth of a stream. Here it heard the voices of ten children who were on the mainland above the beach. Near the place where it heard the voices, the octopus emerged from the sea and began walking on the beach. Now this was not a true octopus but was something very evil. It was a masalai.

It came up to the place where the children were. It approached the children and asked them, "Where are your fathers and mothers? Where did they go?"

The children answered, "They went into the forest to their garden."

Now this Kut, the Octopus, asked them, "At what time will they return?"

The children answered, "When the sun sets, they shall return."

Then Kut, the masalai, asked them, "Do you have any green leafs* for eating in the house? The children answered, "There are some in the house."

Then Kut said to them, "Cut up the green leafs then put them into a pot. Make a very hot fire; put the pot on the fire and cook the leafs." The children made a hot fire and began cooking the leafs. Kut, the Octopus, crawled into the pot with the leafs and the children cooked Kut, the Octopus, with the green leafs. The children cooked and cooked until all was well done.

Kut, the Octopus, said to the children, "I am cooked near to being well done. Now take the pot some distance into the bush and pour it out." The children took the pot into the bush and poured it out.

Then Kut, the Octopus, came to the house and sat at the corner of the door. He asked the children, "Do you have taro in the house of your mother? Get it and eat it together with green plant leafs." They took and ate.

Kut, the Octopus, was sitting at the door. It got some lime and with water made a looking glass. It viewed itself in a mirror-like glass and began combing its hair. It was near the time the fathers and mothers were to return from their garden. Then Kut, the Octopus, went back into the sea. Four days went by; then Kut returned to the place where the children were.

In the meantime the mothers and fathers, having come back from the garden, saw that all their children looked plump and healthy. Their skin was very clean and clear. They said: "You did not look as good as this before we left for the garden."

The children said, "There was a thing that came to us. It took care of us and made food for us. It said to us, "Take the edible leafs and cook me with it.""

Now, the fathers and mothers understood what had happened. All the fathers and mothers went away again except for one man who stayed and hid himself. He said to the children, "At what time did Kut, the Octopus, say he would come back?"

The children spoke, "He is to come at the time it is raining and when a rainbow appears. That is the time Kut is to come." They stayed there until Kut, the Octopus, came again. It came back.

It spoke to the children as it did before, saying, "Do you have leafs in the house like last time?" Kut, the Octopus, stayed by the door. The man came out of hiding. He looked as if he would kill Kut, the Octopus.

Kut, the Octopus, ran toward Lusa, but man cut off one of the legs of Kut and he went into the sea saying to the man, "If you were not here I would have fattened all of your children and then would have devoured all of them. You came now."

The man heard this and went up to the mainland.

*Storyteller: Bilomon Bosiih from Lundret. *Leafs is Pidgin English for leaves.*

A Snake Woman

A certain meri from Western Manus was half human and half snake. From her waist up, she was a human being and from her waist down, she was a snake. To move about, she had to crawl on her belly. However, Samakraapis did not harm anyone or anything. Some people liked her, but most villagers wouldn't come close to her because they didn't like snakes and were afraid.

Somehow, she had ten children, five sons and five daughters. She fed them until they were all grown to adults and were married, all except for the last-born daughter, Niomak, who was left behind with her mother, the centaur woman.

Niomak was the only one of her brothers and sisters who loved their mother. One day Niomak married a man named Sabaundru and Sabaundru didn't like snakes. So, when Niomak got married, her mother wanted to go to live with her first-born son, Koulak. But Koulak said, "No, Mother, because you look so ugly and horrible, you cannot live with me and my family. Go ask Banch, your second-born son. He might accept you to live with him, but not me."

So the poor snake woman crawled on her belly very slowly to her second-born son, Banch, who told her the same thing that Koulak, the first-born son, had told her. Then she crawled to Silih, the third-born son, but he said the same words that Koulak and Banch had told her.

The same thing happened over and over again as she crawled to all of her nine children: Koulak, Banch, Silih, Sabok, Kupe and her four daughters, Bluh, Sol, Siwa and Nioke. They all hated their own mother.

Exhausted and sad, at last the snake woman crawled to Niomak, her last-born daughter who accepted her mother into her home. Niomak told her mother, "Mother, I thought that all of us would look after you because you are now getting to be a very old snake woman. All my older brothers and sisters are filling their greedy minds with their present life. They have forgotten all about their childhood life and how you took care of us, even when you had to crawl on your belly everywhere. Never mind, you are welcome. You may stay here and live with me and my family until your day comes." So Samakraapis, the old snake woman, at last had a place to lay her head and rest. She lived with her last-born daughter for several years, even though Sabaundru was not happy about his mother-in-law living with them.

Some years later, Niomak and Sabaundru had a baby boy. When he was about two years old, one day Niomak put the little boy to bed. She left him at home to stay with his grandmother, the snake woman, while she and Labaundru went to the bush to hunt cus cus.

While they were still in the bush, the little one woke up and began to cry. The old grandmother coiled herself tightly and sat herself in the corner on an old mat, listening. The old meri listened to the little boy crying for a long time. She knew that the boy was frightened of her and would cry louder and louder if she tried to comfort him.

Finally, she became so sorry for him that she left her mat, wiggled over and picked up the boy to cradle him. When the boy recognized his grandmother, he became so frightened that he burst into an even louder cry. He cried for quite a long time; it took him one whole day to cry.

Sometime later that afternoon, when Sabaundru, his father, decided to go home to see if the boy was all right. As he got nearer and nearer, he heard the boy crying loudly. He thought that it was dangerous for his son to cry for such a long time and so loudly. So he hurried to the hut. There he saw his mother-in -law cradling his son in her arms.

"Oh, you ugly, horrible centaur woman, you are frightening my son," cried the man, "Now get yourself away from my son before I can't help but kill you!" Labaundru became so angry that he picked up an axe and chopped his mother-in-law in half.

Niaomak was still in the bush, but as soon as the old snake woman died, her blood left her and crawled to her last-born daughter. "Daughter of mine, I have been killed by your husband, Labaundru." Niaomak left everything and ran home to see what had happened. She arrived home. It was true. Her mother was dead.

She picked snake woman up in her arms, burst into a loud cry and walked around and around the village. It took her two days to cry for her mother. She saw now that all she had in her heart was love for her mother. After a few days of crying, she buried her mother, the old snake woman. Niaomak became so upset and angry about her mother's death that she left her husband with the boy and went to look for a new one.

Storyteller: Caleb Calowon from Loniu.

Cabeb explained about the story, "All along the island of Western Manus are legends about a certain creature who was half woman and half snake. This legend has been told by parents, grandparents and great-grandparents from all the tribes to the present time. These kinds of legends are never forgotten. It is strange for us people when we see creatures such as what you would call a centaur. We can be frightened and try to get away, but sometimes things happen like in this legend."

How Sunbirds Came To Manus

Once upon a time there lived in Loniu a man and his wife. They had many children—five girls and five boys. The children were hungry all the time. The man and his wife worked hard to feed them, but they gulped the food down and were still always hungry. The wife was tired and angry. One day she told her husband, "Take these children far away into the bush and lose them. We cannot feed them anymore."

So the father took them away far into the bush, but one little boy carried stones with him. Every fifteen feet he dropped one stone. By mid-day, the father said, "Stop here. You children stay and I will go hunt for some birds. When I come back, we will go home." But he went the other way and quickly went home.

The children waited and waited until night for their father to return. When the moon came up, the stones shone bright in the moonlight. They followed the path of the shining stones and went home. When they reached the house, the wife was very angry. She told the husband, "You could not have taken them to the bush; maybe you only took them near our house!"

The next day the father again called the children and led them deeper into the bush. This time the little boy couldn't get stones, but had pieces of bread he was eating. He dropped the crumbs along every fifteen feet as he had with the stones.

By mid-day the father said, "Stop here, you children, stay here and I will go hunt for birds. When I come back, we will go home." But again he went the other way and quickly went home.

They waited and waited, but their father did not return. The boy who had dropped the crumbs led his brothers and sisters, but the birds had come and eaten the crumbs. After they had walked a long way, they saw a light in the distance. They followed the light and came to the house of a masalai man. The wife of the masalai was kind to the children because she was their mother's sister. She fed them all they wanted as they were very hungry.

Late that night, the masalai smelled the children and said they he would eat them all that night. When the woman heard her husband say this, she crept into the room where the children were sleeping and exchanged the children's clothes. She put the masalai's children's clothes on the little children and put their clothes on the masalai's children. Later when the masalai went to kill them, he took his axe and chopped his own children. After he unknowingly ate them all, he was tired and went away to sleep.

Early in the morning about three o'clock, the masalai's wife woke the children up, cooked them some sago to eat, and gave them a little knife to protect them from the masalai. The good woman then said magic words to the oldest brother so that anything he met would obey him.

The children walked many miles from Lugos to Momote Airport, twenty miles. In the morning when the sun came up, the masalai noticed the children were gone and realized he had eaten the wrong ones. He was furious and set out after them. He had a long, long step and he almost reached the children in less than two hours.

When he was about a mile away, the children reached a small crab hole. The big brother said his magic words, "If the crab hole belongs to us, it will open wide, but if the crab hole belongs to the masalai, it will not open."

Just then the hole opened wide enough for only one person at a time to go into the door. One by one, all the children scrambled into the opening. When they all got inside, the hole closed behind them. The masalai smelled everywhere, but could not smell the footprints of the children so he went away.

When the children noticed that they did not hear his noises any more, the big brother said some magic words again. The hole opened and the children went out.

That night they were two times as far as twenty-five miles away. They slept under a big tree and waited for morning to come. In the morning, the masalai smelled the tracks and came again to find them. The children had awakened and began to walk again.

When they saw that the masalai was almost up to them, the oldest brother said to a nearby rock, "If you are my rock, you will open up, but if you belong to the masalai, you will not."

The rock opened and the children went inside. The masalai took a stick and began to dig, hoping he would find the children. After a long time without success, the masalai became tired and slept beside the rock. The big brother said the magic words and the rock opened a little bit so he could see out and see what the masalai was doing.

When he saw the masalai was sleeping, he went inside and took his knife. Again he said the magic words and the rock opened big. He crawled out and stuck his knife in the heart of the masalai and pulled the knife all the way to his stomach. He cut out the lung and hung it in the tree. Just then a black bird came and talked to him, "Follow me. I know the way to a little house."

The children followed the black bird and reached a village where an old woman lived who could not see well. The woman said, "Build your house here under this big tree and live with me." But she warned them, "You can use all the trees for firewood but not the special tree in the middle. If you use it, you will change into a sun bird."

Each day they took turns cooking for each other. It came time for the last born, a small brother, to cook the food. He did not use the right trees, but took wood from the tree in the middle. He cooked food and when each one put the food into their mouth, they changed into a sun bird and flew up into the tree crying.

Meanwhile the old woman had a daughter. Every time she came home to her mother, she would ask, "Have I got any brothers or sisters?"

"Yes, you have some," the old woman said.

But the girl wanted to know, "Where are they now?" she asked.

"They are in the bush," the old woman answered.

The girl sewed five pairs of brightly coloured trousers for the boys and five dresses for the girls. When she was finished, she carried the clothes and looked for the children. She came to the tree where the children had changed into sunbirds, but she did not see the children.

When she saw the old woman in her house, she went in and asked the old woman if she had seen the five girls and the five boys. The old woman said, "They have already changed into sunbirds and have flown up into the tree."

The girl went under the tree and threw up the dresses and trousers. As each one put on theirs, they would fly down and stand beside her on the ground. She put her arms around all of them and they went into the old woman's house.

The old woman asked them if they would be her sons and daughters. They all agreed and lived happily ever after.

Storyteller: Lihui from Loniu. Told to her by her mother.

Biboingangdri, A Bad Mama

In a far off time there lived a woman in a village. Her name was Biboingangdri. One day her husband went off into the bush to hunt for kapul. Biboingangdri and the child belonging to her remained in their house. At the time of the sun, the two went to fill up the water tub. When the two finished filling it with water, they closed their eyes and went asleep. After a time, the mother and child went to bathe in the river.

Biboingangdri stayed on the bank while she sent the child belonging to her into the water. The child belonging to her called out, "Look! I am here, Mama."

His mother replied, "Go on a little further."

The child called out again: "I am here."

Her Mama called out, "Go on a little more!"

Now Biboingangdri saw that her child did not go on further into the water. She went and pushed him down in the water. She pushed down the child. Now the child cried, "Mama, Mama."

Biboingangdri said, "You are not a child of mine. Your mother is back in the house."

Then she pushed him down again. This child died; he was dead all the way. Now the woman carried the child out on to the bank. She cut open his bowels. She carried water and came to the house. She cut her child up and cooked him in a saucepan. She cooked taro in a saucepan to go along with her meal.

This man of hers was still in the bush. The woman hurried to get the taro and the meat of the child ready. Now the man came back from the bush. He had caught a pig and a kapul. When he came, he asked the meri belonging to him, "Where is the child belonging to the two of us?"

The woman replied, "The child went to his cousins." Now he sent this woman to get the child.

She came back to the house again without the child. The man again said, "Go and search in another house."

The woman stayed away for a long period of time. The man remained in the house. He smelled that the meat of the child was done. He cried for his son, but there was no one to make his son alive.

The woman came back to her husband. She spoke to him and said, "You, take the food prepared for you and bring it down below." The food had been placed on top of a beam of the house so dogs could not get it. The taro was in one bowl and the boy child was in the other bowl. Now the man spoke, "I will watch. Just eat now."

The man sat down and looked at the woman as she ate the child belonging to her. One time the woman spoke, "I am full. I cannot eat more." The man belonging to her said, "You finish it." So she finished the child and the taro. It was all finished.

He said to her, "Drink two bottles of water now!"

Close to them was the big tub of water. She drank it all. The man went to the men's lodge, the haus boi; the woman wanted to sleep. The woman stayed in the house and made up a mat to sleep on. She lay down and went to sleep on it. He fastened the two doors of the house.

The man stayed in the haus boi. It was now night. In the middle of the night, nearly morning, the woman's belly burst; the man belonging to her heard it. And the men of the village heard the terrible sound of the woman's bursting belly. They asked, "Whose woman is it whose belly has burst?"

"Her name her "Biboingangdri," they said." And so, the man had revenge on his woman, Biboingangdri who had eaten their child and her belly burst.

Storyteller: Boksep from Tingau, a seventy-year old man. Told to him by his grandfather.

A Visit To The King's Palace

A long time ago, there lived a small boy and his older sister. They were all alone since their father and mother had both died. One day they said, "We should go to see the King's palace and visit the King."

When their dead father and mother heard this, they changed their spirits into two dogs, a male and female. So the brother and his sister, together with their dogs, set out on their journey to the King's palace.

They had walked a long way when they came to some men working to build a house. The sister saw one of the men. She liked him and told her brother that she was not going any further. She said, "Brother of mine, I am going to marry that man." The brother tried to persuade her to come with him, but she would not come.

The brother went on alone on his journey to the King's palace. After a while, he came to another place where he saw twenty women. When he told them where he was going, they said, "You must not go to the King's palace. Near the palace, there is a huge masalai. He will eat you. You must stay with us and be safe."

But the brother said, "No, I am going to go to the palace and see this masalai." And he went on.

When he got to the palace, he found the nearby house of the masalai. When he went to the house, there was the King's daughter. She asked him, "Why do you come here?"

He said, "I have heard that a masalai lives near your father's palace. Where is this masalai?"

The King's daughter said, "He already has gone. He went to the bush to find food."

The brother told the girl, "I want to kill this masalai. You must boil water and make it very hot."

Then the brother said, "It's six o'clock now and the masalai is coming. Put me inside the saucepan to hide and put my two dogs near the door."

When the masalai came to the house, he smelled a man. He asked the King's daughter, "Who do I smell? I can smell someone in my house!"

She answered, "Yes, there is a man here. He said he was going to kill you."

The masalai commanded, "Call him here."

So the King's daughter called him. When he came, the masalai said, "Choose the kind of weapons you would like to fight with. We are going to fight—rifle or knife?"

The brother chose the knife and they started to fight. It was a fierce battle, but the boy killed the masalai. He told the King's daughter to put the masalai in a saucepan. He told her to stay here in the house of the masalai. He was going back to see the twenty women he had met on the way. He wanted to tell them he had killed the masalai.

Meanwhile, the King had sent three men to go and get his daughter in the house of the masalai. When they went to the house, they found the masalai was dead. They took the King's daughter home and they lied and said, "Oh King, we have killed the masalai." The King was very happy. He sent a message around the palace that he was going to have a big party. He invited everyone to come to see the three men who had killed the masalai. One would be chosen at the party to marry his daughter.

The party began. The brother and the twenty women heard about the party. They decided to go to the palace to see the party. When they arrived, the King's daughter was standing at the door. She called them to come inside.

When the King saw them, he asked, "Why have you brought those women and that boy inside the house?" She said, "Father, those three men have tricked you. This is the boy that killed the masalai. He is here and I am going to marry him."

The boy's sister had come to the party too. He said, "You didn't come with me when I needed you. You wouldn't come to the King's palace with me. Now you must come to me and be my servant." When she heard this, she began to cry.

Storyteller: Hikabet from Loniu. Told to her by her mother.

One Man, His Wife, And Their Son, A Monkey

O nce upon a time in the Loniu village, there lived a man, Gabriel, and his wife, Hannah. After a while they had a son who was a monkey. When he grew up, he saw a young woman in the village who was very pretty. He said, "I want to marry you."

She answered, "You are not a man. You are a monkey!"

The next time he saw her, again he said he wanted to marry her. Again she said, "You are not a man." The younger sister saw the monkey and agreed to marry him and so she did.

Later at the King's palace, races were to be held. Hannah and Gabriel went to the games and left their son, the monkey, in the house with his wife. The monkey said to his wife, "Go and see the game and I will stay here in the house." When his wife went to the palace, the monkey got out of bed and went to the kitchen. There he changed himself into a man.

He called one white horse, dressed himself, got on the horse and rode to the palace. It was time for the race. The monkey man came in first; all the others were behind him. When the race was finished, the King called for the first and second place people to come and get their prize. When they called for first place, no one answered. So they called second place and the second place winner went and took his prize. The third came too.

When his family came to their house, the monkey asked, "Who won the game?"

His wife said, "One man won, but when the King called him to take the prize, he ran away. I would like to marry that man."

The monkey said, "I am not a man. If you want to marry him, you go and leave me alone."

The next day, they went to the palace again. This time the father and mother went first. The monkey's wife told them, "I will go back and see my husband in the house." But instead, the wife hid herself near the house.

She saw her husband wake up in the bed, go to the kitchen. He took off his monkey skin and changed into a man. His wife said to herself, "Now I know he is really a man and he is tricking me."

When the monkey finished changing himself, he came down and called his white horse. He hopped on and rode again to the King's palace. When he was gone, his wife went into the house and found the husband's monkey skin. She took it down, found some benzene and matches. Then she carried the skin outside, covered it with benzene and struck the match. She burned it. When she finished, she went to the King's palace and watched the game. When the game was finished, her husband again ran home quickly. When he couldn't find his skin in the kitchen, he looked outside and saw the ashes of the fire. He said, "Now I know my wife burned the skin."

When the game was finished, his family came to the house and were surprised to see a man, not a monkey. His wife went to the kitchen and cooked some food. They sat on the verandah and ate their nice food. Then the monkey man asked, "Why did you burn my skin?"

The wife said, "Because I want you to be a man."

The monkey man then explained that he had two fathers. One was a monkey and one was Gabriel. He told her, "Now you have burned my skin, I will have a hard time to get enough money."

When the older sister saw him, she wanted to marry him, but his wife said, "When he was a monkey, you didn't want him. Now that he is a man, you want to marry him, but he is mine."

So the man monkey and his wife lived happily in their house.

Storyteller: Hikabet from Loniu. Told to her by her older sister.

The Lazy Woman

There was once a woman who lived with her husband. They had no children to keep the woman busy so she was often sick. She never helped her husband to work in the garden or to go fishing. Every single day, she would say to her husband, "Oh dear! I cannot help you today."

The husband knew that his wife was very lazy. She liked to dance only with her woman friends. When night came, she would run to the house and sleep on the mat. One day the man told his wife a story about the moon.

The next day the man said, "My dear wife, let's go and work in the garden." The woman was very sad and she went to her room and lay down. "I am very sick, husband," she said. "Soon I am going to die."

The man was very unhappy and went on his way. When he left, she came out of the house and looked around. She saw some women having their bath. She walked to the water and had a bath too. Then she went again with the women and danced until the sun set.

Storyteller: Sarah Pokio from Buliso.

One Day In The Garden

Long ago, there were two sisters living in one village. They were happy and they had a wonderful house to live in. One day they went to their garden to do some work. The younger sister cooked some taro and green leaves. When the food was ready, the younger sister called her big sister to eat.

Before they ate, they went down to the sea to have a bath. The sky was blue and they agreed it was a good day.

They went back to the small cooking house and while they were eating, a big rain came so both of them went to sleep. While they were asleep, a wild dog came along and looked around the garden, but they didn't hear any sounds.

The dog came into the house, killed the youngest sister and began to eat. The older sister heard the bones of her sister crack as the dog chewed. She woke up and opened her eyes, but her sister was not there.

Storyteller: Sarah Pokio from Buliso.

The Masalai And The Breadfruit

Once, there were two brothers and their wives. It came about that the younger brother stayed in the house while the older brother went into the forest to hunt for wild pig. He hunted and hunted but he did not find any wild pigs. He went then to get some breadfruit from a breadfruit tree. He got the breadfruit and brought it home to his wife. His wife cooked the breadfruit. They ate all the breadfruit except for the skin.

They took the skin and wrapped it in leaves. Then they gave the wrapped skin to their child and some of it to the child of his brother as well. The child gave the breadfruit skin to his mother for her to chop up. The children began to cry. They were still hungry.

The father went again into the forest to get some more breadfruit. He came to the tree and climbed up to the top. While he was climbing a leaf fell from the tree very close to the house of a masalai. The masalai saw him at the top of the tree and called out, "Who are you? You there at the top of my tree, who are you?"

The man called back: "It is me. I hear you calling me. I can hear you here up in the tree." Still, the masalai called and called and called to the man in the tree. Other men called; the leaves called; the trees called; the ground called. The man in the tree heard it all.

He said, "There are many of you calling to me. I am only one." He threw the breadfruit to the ground. He threw everything he had to the ground.

He had caught a pigeon which he also threw to the ground. The masalai ran after the pigeon. The man came down from the tree and began to gather the breadfruit that was on the ground. The masalai came; he wanted the breadfruit. The two began to fight. They fought and fought for a very long time.

His brother, back at the house, asked the children, "Where is your father? Where did he go?"

They told him, "He went back into forest to the breadfruit tree to get some breadfruit." The man went into the forest until he came to place where his brother was. When he arrived, he saw his brother fighting with the masalai. He saw his brother was nearly dead. He called to him, "Stop."

He then went and fought with masalai. He prevailed over the masalai and killed him. The brothers took the breadfruit and returned to their house.

Storyteller: Bilomon Bosiih from Lundret.

Papi, Pelai And Cheenin, A Masalai

One day, two men from Loniu, Papi and Pelai, were making plans to go on a fishing trip to catch a big shark. While they were talking, an evil spirit named Cheenin was hiding behind the house of Papi. When Pelai was ready to leave, Papi said, "In the morning when you see the light break, you come to my house to get me and we will go together to catch the shark."

The next morning before Pelai arrived, Cheenin changed himself to look like Pelai and called Papi to wake up. They pulled the canoe to the beach and put it in the water. Papi sat in front and Cheenin sat in the back. They paddled to Lou Island. When they came near to Lou, Papi looked back and was surprised to see Cheenin sitting there and not his friend, Pelai. Cheenin said, "I am going to kill you!" Papi was very frightened and felt sorry for himself, as he did not want to die.

When they reached Lou, Cheenin broke the canoe into little pieces and left Papi on the beach while he went to bring his friend to help kill Papi. While he was gone, a dog came along. "Why do you come to our island?" the dog asked. Papi told him all about how Cheenin had tricked him into thinking he was his good friend, Pelai, and that now he was going to be killed by the two evil spirits.

So the dog said, "You stay here. I will go and get more dogs and we will help you." The dogs came from the village and hid near the road. When the two evil spirits came to get Papi, the dogs jumped out and there was a fierce battle.

Finally, Cheenin, the evil spirit, and his friend were both killed.

The dogs said to Papi, "Come and we will go to our village." Papi didn't know what Cheenin had done with his friend, Pelai, and was very sad. But the dogs were good to him and so Papi lived there happily for some time with the dogs.

One day the dogs said, "We will take you to your village in our canoe." When they brought him to Loniu, at first the people refused to believe it was Papi. They said "Em he die finis long tim before."

So then the dogs brought Papi to his family's haus. They were so happy to see him. All the village made a big feast and had a sing sing to show him how happy they were that Papi had returned to the village.

Storyteller: Hikabet from Loniu. Told to her by her mother.

Masusu's Tower

Once a very long time before even our grandfathers were born, there lived all alone near the village of Tingau, a giant of a Tambaran man, Masusu.

One late afternoon, Masusu was huddled in his house, alone and very cold. It was the "time belong rain" and he wished that the sun could penetrate the clouds, reaching through the lush vegetation surrounding his village and warm his old bones. It was then that Masusu thought of a plan. He would build a tower, a tower of stones that would reach to the sky. Then he could sit in his tower and put his back against the sun and warm himself.

Early the next morning, he arose and searched for just the right spot on which to build his tower. After nearly a day of tramping the hills and valleys near Tingau, he found it—a perfect place near the top of a high mountain, already a good start on his way to the sky.

Every morning after that, Masusu would rise very early and walk through the bush and along the beach, looking for the largest stones in all of Manus. He would carry them one by one to his chosen site for the tower. When he had a large collection, he began to build. Carefully, he placed one stone on top of another. The tower slowly grew skywards. As it grew, its shadow fell into the valley below.

Now, there was another man who lived all alone near the Tingau River. This Tambaran man was an old enemy of Masusu. They had had many quarrels before. One day,

Masusu's enemy too shivered in the cold. He wondered why he did not feel the sun on his back as before; the sun was surely shining. Looking up, he spied the stone tower of Masusu. He was angry. He too wanted the warm sun to fall on his house, and now the tower's shadow was all that fell down to his valley.

The next morning as Masusu was busy searching for more stones, he was unaware of his enemy's new anger. He was unaware that his tower was in danger. Masusu's enemy strode to the mountain where the tower stood and began to climb; he climbed beyond. He put his foot on a huge boulder resting near the top of the mountain above the unfinished stone tower. His voice roared out over the mountain and down through the valleys to Masusu, "All of your stones will fall and be scattered over the mountainside. But my stones, they will stand where I command."

Upon hearing the voice of his enemy, Masusu tried to climb back up the mountain to stop the foot of his enemy and the destruction of his tower. Too late; the boulder crashed down the mountainside, gathering speed as it rolled. His carefully planned tower exploded down the mountainside, scattering huge stones far and wide. Only a few stones were left to mark the site of his hard work.

Masusu was sad. Still cold, he decided not to return to his house near Tingau. Finding a special stone, he shoved it in his anus. He fastened two leaves from the coconut tree on his shoulders and away he flew. He flew and flew until he reached the very top of the mountain. He stayed there, living at Sabon on Top.

One of the stones fell at Poluso and many scattered along the Tei Et River where yet today they remain to remind the people that Masusu's tower almost reached the sun.

Storyteller: Helen Bidrou from Tingau. Told to her by her father who would tell his children many stories of Masusu in the evenings before sleep.

When the Americans arrived during the war, they surveyed the area for the ideal spot for a radio communications tower. Strangely enough, two partial towers now stand side by side, a pile of huge stones and a rusting, abandoned steel structure, both are located on top of the highest mountain around, not far from the village of Tingau.

PART II

Scenes From Around Manus Island

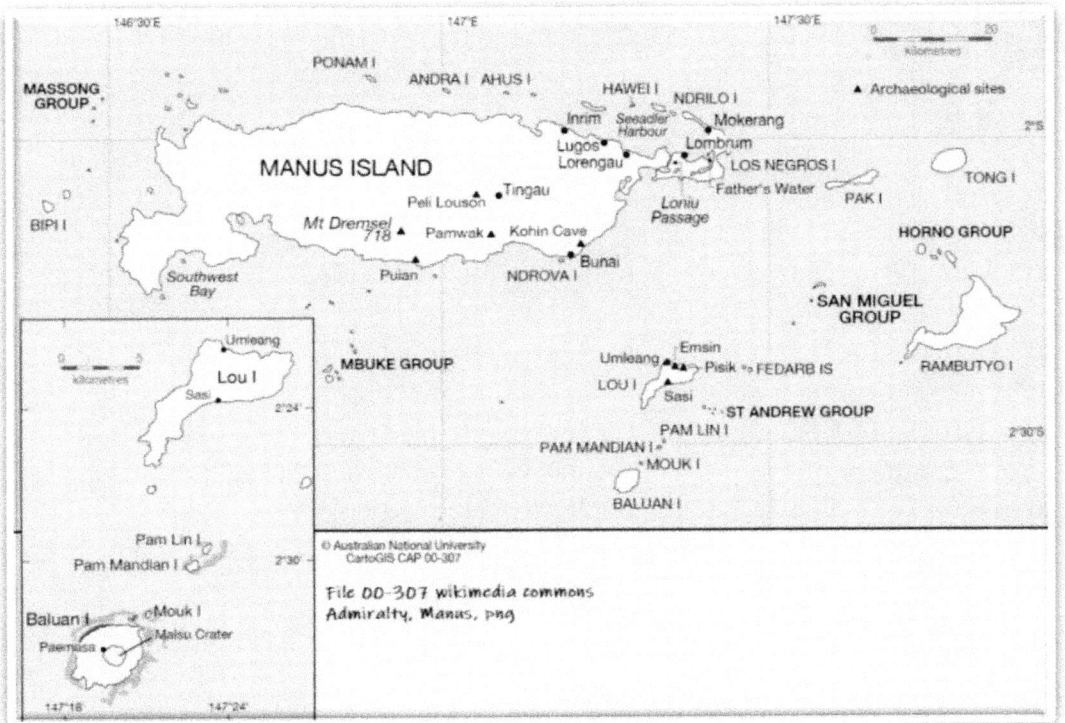

© Australian National University
CartoGIS CAP 00-307

File 00-307 wikimedia commons
Admiralty, Manus, png

Paddling Back Home

Tide's Out

Wash Day in Pond Upriver

Setting the Net

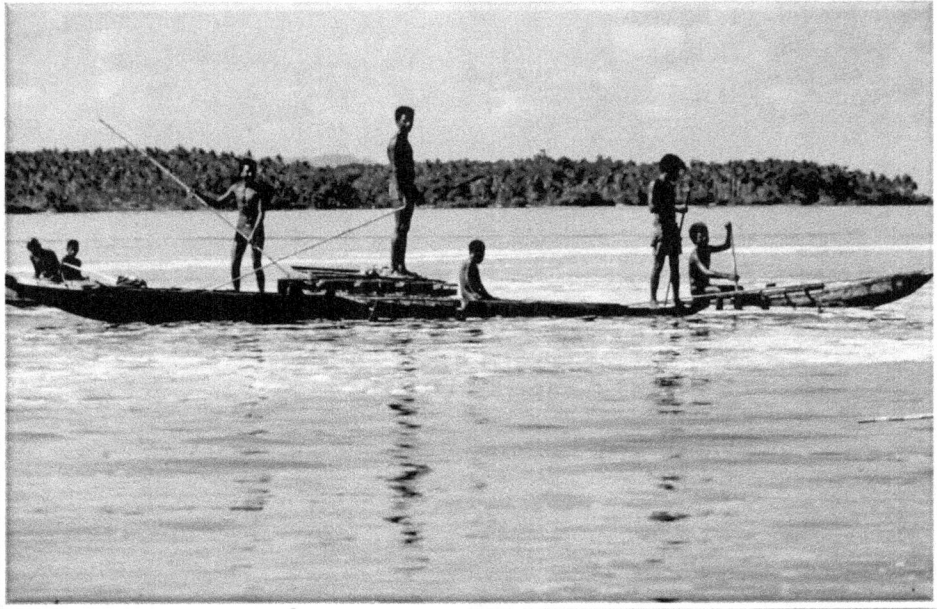

At Home on the Sea

Open Air School

Big Catch

Home Away from Home

Practicing Their English

Wash Day, Bilomon Bosiih

Matthew Bill, Indigenous Teacher, and Family

Bath Time

Bag of Sak Sak Is Hard Work

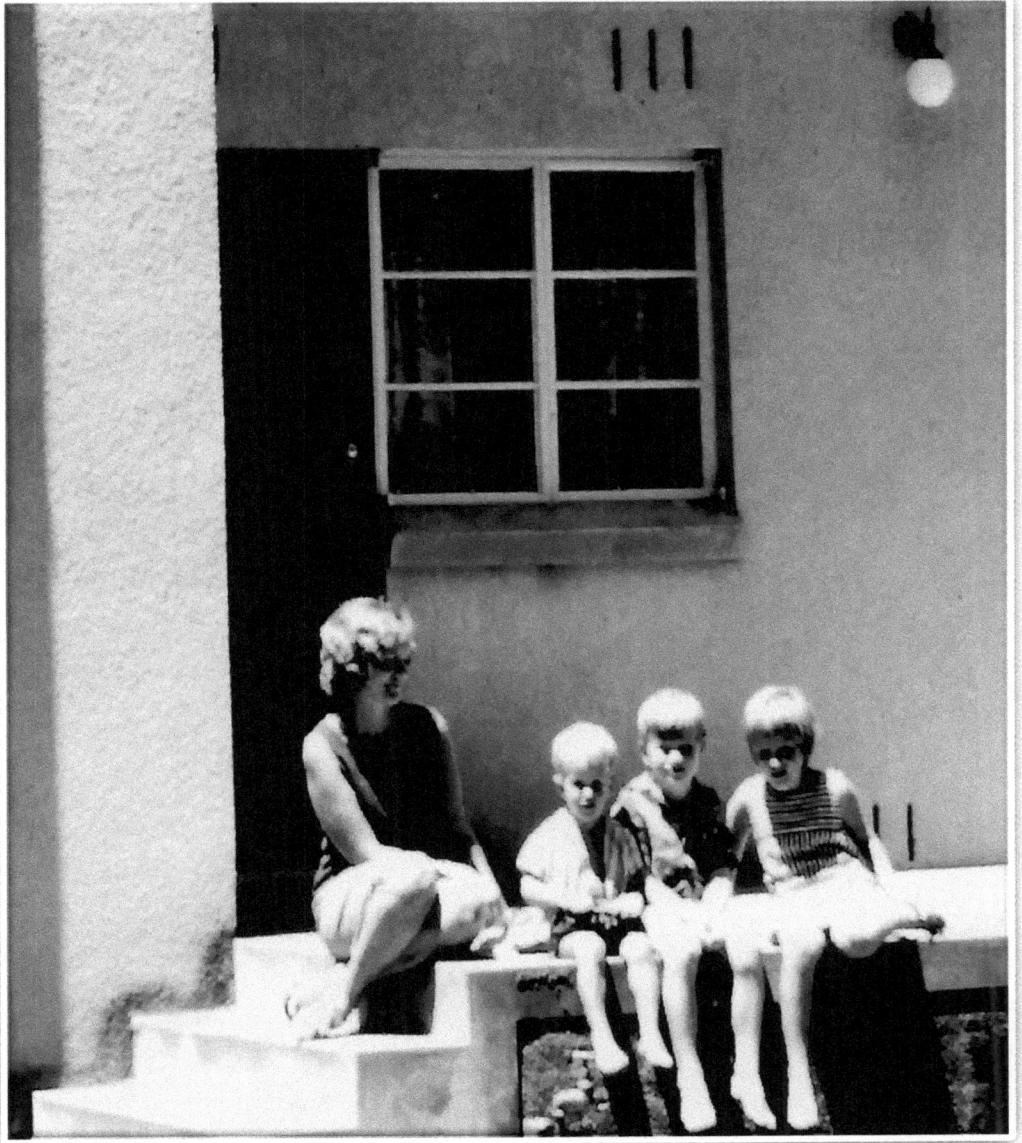

Sad Farewell to Manus Island

PART III

Tales Told By Manus Island Sixth Graders

How The Masalai Was Killed

Long ago, there lived in Tumoh, a grandmother and her granddaughter. They were very poor. The people in the village didn't want to look after them. So the grandmother said, "Let's pack our things and go and live in the bush." They carried their belongings and walked away. They found a clearing and started to build their house.

When the house was finished, they put the things inside. The next morning, they made a garden for themselves. They planted some taro tops. The next day the taro tops had already grown. They took some taros and cooked them. They slept that night. When morning came, they saw a huge pig eating their taro tops. They chased the pig away. The pig did this several times. Then one afternoon the grandmother said, "We'll dig a big hole in the middle of the garden." They both worked together and the hole was finished immediately. They carried some taros home and cooked them. When the pig came, it fell into the hole. The grandmother killed the pig and carried it up out of the hole.

They didn't know that the pig was a masalai pig. They carried the pig home and started to cook it. Then the head of the pig said, "Today I'll eat you and your grandmother."

They were afraid and ran away to Pohyamore. There they found a man by the name of Pokop. He told them to go inside. Then Pokop said, "I'll dig a hole and put some sharp spears inside. I'll put a ladder over top. Your job is to boil water and put stones inside the pot."

Then he chopped the legs of the ladder in half. When the masalai came, it danced on the ladder. The ladder broke and down went the masalai into the hole. They poured the hot water on top of him and masalai was dead.

The grandmother, the granddaughter and Pokop lived happily ever after.

Storyteller: Paul Makis from Ndranou.

How the Masalai Was Killed

A Stolen Girl

One beautiful day a young girl was walking along the path to the garden. She was singing as she went. Far above in the top of a tall casuarina tree, there stood the monster of the cave.

The monster flew down and carried the young girl away to its home. On their way to the monster's cave, they saw a monkey who was sitting on the branch of a huge tree. The monkey said to the monster, "What is that you are carrying, Monster?"

The monster said, "I am carrying my daughter. She was lost and now I have found her." When the girl heard this, she was very frightened but couldn't say anything.

The young girl's parents were waiting for her at home. Her parents were the King and Queen. One day the King called all the soldiers and told them to go and look for their daughter. The King told one man by the name of Tim to lead them to the bush.

While they were walking through the bush, they saw a monkey. The monkey said to them, "Who are you looking for?"

Tim answered him, "We are looking for the King's daughter." The monkey showed them the way to the cave and they went inside. While they were walking inside the cave, they heard a loud noise from a monster.

Tim was the first one who saw the monster and gave a signal to his soldiers to fire their rifles. Tim went, "One, two, three, fire!" And they fired their rifles. They killed the monster and brought the King's daughter home safely.

Storyteller: Poyasei Ndohnum from Warabe.

A Stolen Girl

Spirit Of The Masalai

Once a young girl was sent to the garden to plant taro. When she was in the garden, she put her basket down. She went and dug a hole for the taro. She planted the taro and then she was ready to go home. She took some food with her.

When she was going home along the path, far above in the top of a tall casuarina tree sat a huge monkey. It wasn't a monkey; it was a masalai that had changed himself into a monkey. The young girl didn't know that it was a masalai. So she carried the monkey and took it home to her parents.

When she told her parents about it, they decided that it could stay and they looked after the monkey very nicely. But one day they did not feed the monkey. Then when they were away in their garden, the monkey changed himself back into a masalai and ate up all their food. Then he changed himself to a monkey again and went in a very deep sleep.

In the afternoon when the family came home from their garden, they found there wasn't anything in the house. This caused them to kill the monkey. Later on, everything was in good condition. So they lived in their village happily ever after.

Storyteller: Potuwan Peion from Laues.

Spirit of the Masalai

Young Girl And The Cus Cus

One day in the top of a tall tree, there sat a cus cus. A young girl didn't see the cus cus as she was singing and walking to the garden.

When she got to the garden, she put her basket down and started to plant her taro. When she had planted her taro, the rain began to fall down.

Then she went to her small house in her garden. She cooked her taro in the small house in her garden. Then she put all the taro in the basket and started to go back home.

She was walking slowly towards home when the cus cus jumped and sat on top of her basket. Her basket fell down with the cus cus on top. She started to run home. She ran and ran very, very quickly home and told what had happened.

They let the cus cus sit on top of the basket until they became hungry. Then they cooked him. The cus cus was a good meal.

Storyteller: David Stoga from Tingau.

The Young Girl and the Cus Cus

Crocodile Rescues The Girl

One day a young girl was walking along a path. She was going to the garden. Far above in the top of a tall casuarina tree, she saw a huge snake. When she saw the snake crawling quickly down the tree and coming toward her, she cried out for help.

A crocodile heard her and came running toward the girl. When the crocodile saw that the snake wanted to eat the girl, the crocodile ate the snake.

She was very happy when she saw that the crocodile rescued her. She told the crocodile, "I will take you to my house. I will give you some gold because you helped me. When the snake wanted to eat me, I called for help and you came hurrying to help me."

Storyteller: Stephen Sobokabun from Lesau.

Crocodile Rescues the Girl

Gathering Coconuts

Long, long ago there were two brothers living on an island. They both were living happily on the island, but then the older brother said, "Now brother, we are going to another island to pick some coconuts of our own and carry them home."

They went to the beach and pulled their canoe into the sea. They paddled and paddled for a long time before they reached the shore of the island where the coconuts grew. The youngest brother threw the anchor down. They both went to the plantation and got as many coconuts as they wanted.

They carried all the coconuts that they had collected to the beach. They put all the coconuts in the canoe until it was overfilled. They pulled up the anchor and began paddling on and on until they came to the middle of the sea. Suddenly the canoe turned over and the oldest brother threw all the coconuts out. He poured out the water from the canoe. When he finished, he hopped in and paddled away. He left his younger brother drifting.

The small brother gathered all the coconuts and tied them together. Then he sat on top of all the coconuts and paddled with his two hands. He paddled and paddled until he reached the shore. He climbed off and carried all the coconuts to the land.

He was tired. He wanted to rest, but he saw some vegetables behind a tree. As he walked towards the tree, he saw that it was his father's garden when he was still alive. He went to sleep under the tree. While he was sleeping, he dreamed about his brother finding him.

He suddenly woke up and said to himself, "At first he forgot me and went away. Now I must find my way home." He ran through the thick bushes and came to the house. He knocked on the door and the door opened. When he entered, the Masalai chopped off his neck, and that was the end of his trip for coconuts.

Storyteller: Simon Pokus from Tingau.

Gathering Coconuts

The First Feast

Once upon a time there was a village on the coast of Manus. One day the chief's wife called her daughter to go fishing. They walked a long way and sat down to rest by a bigpella stone. It was a masalai, not a stone.

A masalai had seen them coming and changed himself into a stone that could talk. When the chief's wife asked questions, the stone answered. She was afraid. She told her daughter to take their basket and hide in it.

After a long time, the chief's wife speared a fish and thought she would go home. She called for her daughter, but no answer came.

The masalai went away to his house. He carried the basket with the child inside. When he got home, he ate the child. The chief's wife got home and told her husband about the sad news. The village men went to the bush with their dogs, axes, spears and kaparesas.

They found the masalai sound asleep, his belly full. They killed the masalai and took out the chief's daughter.

The chief made lots of food for the people and they called it The First Feast.

Storyteller: Lihieu Elisha from Loniu.

The First Feast

The Government Man

The village men sat in the government house. They were there for thinking about their land that the government wanted to buy from them.

After a long time, when all the men had agreed to sell, one lapun turnbrow slowly stood up. He spoke, "No, because if we sell the land, we will have no land for our children when they grow up." He was a good man and thought of his children.

The government man was very unhappy with the old lapun turnbrow. The government man needed to earn his money. He went to another village to ask them for their land. He asked them if they agreed to sell it to the government.

They also did not agree with him and he was very sad. In his heart he thought about going home without earning his money. And without buying the land belonging to the villagers.

Storyteller: Peter Pou-uh from Sirrah.

The Government Man

The Old Widow And The Eagle

Long, long ago there was a widow. She had no sons or daughters. She lived in the bush by herself.

One day while she was working in her garden. She wanted to clear the sugarcane. As she did this, the leaf of the sugarcane cut her finger. Blood came out and she put it in the shell of a coconut and covered it with the leaf of the paw paw tree. Then she went home.

A week later, she came back to the garden. She looked in the shell of the coconut. To her surprise, the blood had turned into a tiny bird. She called it Eagle. She took Eagle home with her and looked after it. It grew bigger and bigger.

It went to the sea to fish for them and both lived happily in their home.

Storyteller: Samuel Madusabai from Lesau.

The Old Widow and the Eagle

The Crocodile

Two young brothers were fishing on the river. They did not see the huge crocodile watching from the water's edge. It swam slowly toward them but still they didn't see it. So it crept up to the canoe and turned it over. The crocodile caught the first brother on the legs. It started to pull him down to the sea.

The other brother was surprised to see what had happened. He picked up the big stick and threw it at the crocodile's head, but the crocodile was still carrying the boy.

The boy in the crocodile's mouth also tried hard to get away from the crocodile's mouth but he couldn't. With a loud cry, the second brother paddled the canoe home and told the village people about what had happened.

So they all rushed with their canoes toward the boy and the crocodile. But when they went there, there was nothing but blood. So they went back home sadly. They carried the huge crocodile home and cooked it for their dinner.

Storyteller: Pangai Samuel from Loniu. Very similar crocodile stories were told by James and Keheng from Loniu, Palawa from Ndranou and Sipose from Nihon.

The Crocodile

The Old Woman And Her Cousin

Long, long ago, there lived an old woman and her cousin. They lived in Polnuwom. There they made their garden. A wild pig went and ate their taro. They were very angry at the pig. So they went to another village and told all the men to go in the garden and kill the pig.

Then all the men went to the garden and killed the pig. The old woman said, "We want only the head of the pig. The body you carry is yours." The old woman and her cousin cooked their pig's head. She told her cousin to stay and guard the head.

The old woman went to the garden to get some taro. While she was at the garden, the pig's head said, "Today I will eat you and the old woman." They were very frightened. They left the pig's head in the pot and ran away to another village.

They walked and walked until they reached Tulul. Then they stopped. An old woman was making a magic basket. She made one basket and blew it to different villages, but it was not right. So she blew the second time and this time she blew the basket to Pohyomore.

In Pohyomore, there lived Pokop, a lapun man, and his wife. Then Pokop said to the basket, "Go and tell the old woman and her cousin to come to us." They came to Pokop's family and lived there safely. After a while, they wanted to go back home.

That morning, the pig's head changed to a masalai. The masalai followed the old woman and her cousin until it came to Polnuwom where they lived. There he ate both of them. Just like he said he would.

Storyteller: Tawe from Ndronou.

The Old Woman and Her Cousin

A Girl And A Bird

The bird was sitting on the top of the tree and singing. When a girl heard the bird singing, she was very sad. She wanted to climb up the tree to hold the bird.

When she climbed the tree, the bird flew far away and sat on a rock. The girl followed it. When she got to the rock, the bird flew far away and sat on the top of the mountain. She followed it again. She went so far that she stood on the top of the mountain. And the bird cried out again.

She heard it. She wanted to follow it, but she was very tired. She sadly walked back home.

Storyteller: Dorcas Kanat from Bowat.

A Girl and a Bird

The Ten Men Who Wanted To Go Fishing

Long, long ago, there were ten men who lived in a little house near the beach of Buka. With those ten men, there was a man with a crooked leg. One day the crooked-legged man said, "We'll go to the bush and cut some bamboo for spears."

They went into the bush and cut some bamboo. After cutting the bamboo, they went home. There they sat down and started to make their spears. All of them made spears by themselves. Only that man with a crooked leg, he didn't. He asked and asked each of those nine men to fix his spear, but they wouldn't help him. He asked and asked, but the same thing happened. So he just made his own spear.

When he finished, they all went fishing. When they were fishing, all of the fish were caught by that crooked-legged man.

All of a sudden, he said, "We'll go home."

They went home and cooked the fish and ate them. There they lived happily at home on the beach of Buka.

Storyteller: Sion Papi from Loniu.

The Ten Men Who Wanted to Go Fishing

To The Bank

One afternoon a boy named Malum came running down the track towards the river bank. He walked beside the bank and then he stood.

He heard a small cry coming out from the river bank. He stood thinking and talking quietly to himself, and then said, "I must go and see what that strange noise is."

He walked closer and closer and he could hear the sound real clear. He thought to himself, "It might be the monster of the bank."

He began walking quickly along the bank. Suddenly, a big huge monster came out of a hole in the bank and said, "Little boy, come here. Who told you to come here? I'm going to eat you!"

"Oh!" cried the boy, and he started running again. He was running so fast that no ordinary animal could catch him, not even a horse. He kept on running up the track, up the hill and down the valley.

But, at last the huge monster caught him with his long fingernails.

Storyteller: Jerry Daniel from Buliso.

To the Bank

Two Brothers Go Hunting

Long ago there were two young brothers who lived in the village. One day they decided to go hunting. Early in the morning they got their spears and walked away. When they were on their way to cross the river, a man from another village shot the younger one in his neck.

Then he called out, "Brother, brother, come back, a man shot me on my neck." When his brother turned his eyes back, he saw a man running on the other side of the river.

The older brother swam across the river and ran after him, killing him on the other side of the river. On his way back, he saw his younger brother running behind him.

Then they both came back to their village.

Storyteller: Pokela Abraham from Lundret.

Two Brothers Go Hunting

Two Brothers Meet A Bird

Once there were two brothers who lived in their home far from town. One day they got up and talked to each other. They were talking about going swimming. The biggest brother said to his little brother, "Go to the house and get all the things for swimming."

When all things were ready, they started to walk to the beach. After swimming, they started walking back. As they were going home, they saw a bird's nest and said to each other, "Tonight we'll come here and catch it."

When the night came, the two brothers came with a bus rop. The bird talked to them, "Who are you? Go home now or else I'll eat you."

So they went back a little way, then the big brother said to his little brother, "You try to see it again." As soon as the brother went to the bird, the biggest brother ran home.

The bird flew after the little brother. The little brother ran to the river but the bird flew faster and stole him.

At last the people from his home came to help him. The bird said, "Tomorrow the two of them will be killed." At last the day came, but it was the bird who was dead.

Storyteller: Puis Sion from Ndronou.

Two Brothers Meet a Bird

Two Young Brothers And Crocodile

Two young brothers were fishing near the bank of the river. They did not see the huge crocodile watching from the water's edge. They were fishing and fishing until the sun set. There was a big storm coming towards them. They were very frightened of the storm coming.

It was dark and all the things seemed to be strange. Two young brothers paddled their canoe but it couldn't go. They were caught by the crocodile with the long sharp teeth. The crocodile turned their canoe over and swallowed the two young brothers.

When the crocodile went home, she opened her mouth and let the two young brothers inside her house. They were very happy inside the crocodile's house enjoying themselves. Mother crocodile told them, "If you are hungry, you'll go to my garden and pick all the sugarcane and vegetables. But I tell you, do not break any branches from the red tree. If you break it, I will be dead and you will be dead too!"

One day the older brother said to his younger brother, "We will escape tomorrow." The older brother went to the bush and cut the huge tree down. And next day they went and dragged it into the water and left it there. When it got dark, the two young brothers woke up from their beds and started to walk away. They were very happy and paddled their canoe home.

Storyteller: Popan Jumogot from Loniu.

Two Young Brothers and Crocodile

Asap And Kanua

Long, long ago there was a girl named Asap. She was the nicest and most beautiful girl in the whole of Manus. Many men wanted to marry her, but she didn't want to. She said, "Sori nogut." She said it over and over. She said sori nogut to all the men who wanted her.

One day Kanua was combing his hair. Then his auntie told him, "You are combing your hair, but you won't be able to marry Asap."

After he combed his hair, he walked along the path to the beach. There he saw one stick drifting on the sea. Kanua said, "If you are a man, come to the shore."

Then Kanua told the stick, "Go to Pabuuan." The stick drifted to Pabuuan where the girl lived. There were many girls, all standing on the shore. Kanua said to the stick, "Go to Asap."

The stick came to Asap because she too had been combing her hair. Asap jumped on the stick and came to Kanua.

They were married. After that, they had one son and they lived happily in their life.

Storyteller: Nahina Pokop from Laues.

Asap and Kanua

Fishing In The River

One day a man and his son went fishing in the river. At the river they caught plenty of fish. His son was tired and wanted to sleep. His father told him, "You stay here and I'll go over there and come back later."

While his father was away, the gigantic monster came along and grabbed the son and ate him up. Then the monster talked to the stone that the boy had sat on. He said, "If his father comes back and calls his son, you must answer his question."

In a few moments, his father called out, "Are you there?" The stone answered, "I am here." When his father came, his son was not there. He cried and went home.

At home he told all the village people what had happened. They took all their spears and knives and went to the river. At the river, they saw the gigantic monster lying in the top of a tree. His stomach was big.

The people cut the tree down and killed the monster. They took the boy out of his stomach. They carried the poor little boy home, but he was dead. They buried him.

Storyteller: Thomas Maien from Loniu.

Fishing in the River

Escape From The Masalai

One dark night, two men decided to go fishing. They took their spears and a tilly lamp and walked to the beach. When they arrived at the beach, they pushed their canoe into the water. They paddled their canoe towards the open sea. There they started fishing on the reef. They fished and fished until nearly midnight.

Suddenly a masalai turned himself into a big shark. He sent a big wave over the canoe. It put their tilly lamp out. Then the masalai swam back to the island. On the island it changed itself into a man. Then he lit a fire and dried himself.

The two men in the canoe saw that fire and they thought they should have a fire too. They paddled their canoe towards the island where the fire was. Closer and closer they went to the island. They anchored their canoe on the shore and walked up towards the fire.

Then the masalai grabbed both of them at once. He put them in prison for a week and then the masalai decided that he would eat both of them. These men heard that the masalai was going to eat them. They found their way out of the cave that the masalai used for his prison house. They escaped and walked back home.

The village people were happy to see them again.

Storyteller: Saliau from Ndnanou.

Escape from the Masalai

Windy Night

It was a dark windy night. Two girls were asleep in their house. Suddenly they woke up shivering. There was a strange noise coming from the bush. It sounded like a wild beast walking around searching for food. The sound was coming closer and closer.

Suddenly they heard a voice saying, "The village is quiet." Then they saw lines of men coming with torches and some other weapons. As the men raised the fiery torches, tears came running down from the girls' eyes. The men stopped and had some food.

The two girls ran out of the house and all around the village to tell what was happening. But the villagers were already getting ready to fight the other men. Then the villagers ran towards the strangers and started to fight. Some boys found stones and started to shoot them too.

After a time, the strangers were tired and ran away to their own village. The village was now free.

Storyteller: Porak from Loniu.

Windy Night

The Masalai And The Dog

Long ago, two sisters lived in a little village on Manus Island. Their house was on the beach. They had worked with their mother in the garden and were very tired. They went to bed and were asleep on their mat of pandanus leaves. Their dog was sleeping with them.

Suddenly the sisters woke up. They were very cold and were shivering. They heard a very strange noise coming from outside the house. They ran outside and saw a huge man coming towards them. It really wasn't a man. It was a masalai.

When it came closer and closer, the two girls ran back into the house, but their dog was left outside. That huge masalai came and took their dog away.

In the morning, the two girls went outside. They could not find their dog. He was gone. They only saw a footprint.

Storyteller: So-onless from Lesau.

The Masalai and the Dog

The Masalai

One day far above in the top of a tall casuarina tree, there sat a masalai. He saw a little girl walking along a path to the garden.

The masalai said, "Where are you going, little girl?" The girl looked around but couldn't see anything. Then she looked up above her head and saw the masalai sitting on the branch of the casuarina tree.

She turned around and ran as quickly as she could back home. She was out of breath when she reached her house. Her mother asked her, "What is the matter?" She said, "I saw a masalai sitting on the casuarina tree."

Her mother told her never to go near the casuarina tree any more.

Storyteller: Ruth Hitahat Polume from Loniu.

The Masalai

Ode To The Manus Island Of 1971

I and my surroundings were one.
I may've lived in a cinder block house,
There on that tropical isle
But the doors and windows were open,
Wide open,
And I was free to merge with my surroundings.

Like small fishes swimming
In and out of a submerged war tank,
No barriers confined me;
Outside and inside melded
With ebb and flow of tidal breezes.

On Manus, that tropical isle,
Palm trees beckoned with outstretched arms;
Gentle breezes skipped over the water
The rhythmic wash of water on sand
Emphasized the slow, unhurried pace of life.

To rush, to be irritated, to be annoyed
Was out of character
With my surroundings,
My tranquility,
My pace, my peace.

My tropical paradise, for a time.

Geneva Ensign

Tok Pisin English

Betel Nut: addictive nut, when chewed with stick dipped in slaked lime powder, gives a "high" and turns mouth and teeth red.

Bigpella: usually meaning "big head," full of himself.

Bilas: decorations on the body, especially traditional decorations such as necklaces, shells, teeth.

Bilum: woven string basket with long straps which are suspended from their heads so hands are free for other work.

Blew it: to work magic.

Breadfruit: a starchy stable of the diet, has to be cooked, sometimes ground for flour.

Bus Rop: rope for using in the bush.

Bus: unsettled wilds of Manus, forests.

Buskanaka: a person who follows a traditional rather than modern lifestyle.

Casuarina Tree: similar to pine but wood is very hard, used for fuel, carving shields, clubs, and masks.

Chauka Bird: a grouse-like bird, also called a Friar Bird.

Cheenin: a masalai; also a name for quinine.

Cus Cus: a small animal that mainly eats leaves fruits, small birds and reptiles. Sometimes kept as a pet until it is killed and eaten.

Flying Fox: in the bat family, often known as a fruit bat.

Gumu: a fern-like plant growing beside the river.

Haus Boi: a house for only the males of a village.

Haus Sik: hospital or clinic.

Kai Kai: general name for food.

Kaparesa: sharp weapon, like a razor blade, sometimes attached to long handle.

Kapul: a small possum-like animal hunted for its meat.

Karoke: a rain mat made from pandanas leaves.

Kau Kau: Papua New Guinea sweet potato.

Kros: angry, upset.

Kulau: fresh green coconut milk.

Lap Lap: long piece of colourful cloth that is wrapped around the waist, like a skirt. Both women and men wear it.

Lapun: meaning old.

Lapun Papa: meaning grandfather.

Lapun Papa Tru: meaning very old grandfather.

Leafs: spinach-like edible fern.

Lus: elongated wooden food dish.

Mango: oval shaped fruit, usually yellowish-green in color.

Masalai: evil spirit, lives in water holes, waterfalls, bends in the river. Can change themselves into snakes, crocodiles and other creatures. May use magic to trick people. Similar to the ogre in Jack and the Beanstalk.

Masusu: name of a Tambaran Man, a guardian spirit.

Meri: girl or woman, yangpella meri is a young girl.

Pandanus Tree: produces fruit that contains a protein-rich seed eaten raw or roasted.

Papait: to work love magic.

Papaya: oval fruit, usually yellow with red flesh.

Paw Paw: large round fruit, yellow inside.

Pidgin English: a trade talk, mixture of local language and English.

Ples Tok: Pidgin English.

Sago: a starch extracted from the spongy centre of palm trunks, is a major staple food, also called rabia and sagu.

Sak Sak: same as sago.

Sap Sap: juice from a plant or working in the garden.

Sing Sing: a gathering together to sing.

Skul: school.

Sori Nogut: a refusal.

Spirits: ghosts of dead people.

Tambaran Man: a male spirit that acts as a guardian, uses magic.

Taro: a starchy potato-like root with edible leaves. Leaves and root must be cooked. If raw, they are toxic.

Tilly Lamp: another name for a kerosene lamp.

Tok Pisin: Pidgin English.

Trochus: a sea snail shell.

Turnbrow: a mild rebel, one who questions.

Win Haus: small hut built in gardens for protection from rain, wind and a place where a cooking fire can be built.

In The Time Before

Matthew Bill

www.ingramcontent.com/pod-product-compliance
Lightning Source LLC
Chambersburg PA
CBHW080516090426
42734CB00015B/3078